Dumbleto

The Story of a Victorian Country House

By John Richard Hodges

John Richard Hodges

For Nick - *A Remarkable Young Man-1979-1998*

There are many people

who come and go in our lives,

a few touch us in ways

that change us forever.

You have made a difference

in my life and I am grateful.

John Richard Hodges ~ 2014

Contents

Foreword

I first went to Dumbleton in the 1960s on a Post Office training course, pleasantly surprised that it was to be in such an impressive country house setting. The view from the drive struck me immediately, especially the low sunlight warming the Cotswold stone against the background of the hills beyond. Itt looked like a house with history behind it.

Forty years later I had the opportunity to be elected to the board of Dumbleton Hall owners, the Post Office Fellowship of Remembrance. It was a privilege to join as a minor successor to a considerable number of hardworking people, too many to mention, who since the 1930s had given so much time, voluntarily to honouring and preserving the memory of 12,850 GPO staff who had been killed in the Two World Wars.

I discovered that Dumbleton had no archive as such, and other than a few notes not much of its history was on record, so I set about some research, even thinking I might write a book one day.

I soon realised that each line of research opened up new topics to investigate, and that the diligence, patience and discipline needed to put it all together was going to be more than I had envisaged! So I came to a compromise and put the most interesting elements into a modest format that could be displayed in the hotel itself. Others took the material and displayed it in a professional style consistent with modern country house decor and the guests seemed to appreciate the information. That was then going to be that. However the information displayed does raise interest. As a Dumbleton Hall 'Archivist', I would get enquiries from people doing their own research. Sometimes I could help, and sometimes they added to our archive material.

One of these enquiries came from a man we have been looking for all along – John Richard Hodges. He contacted us at Dumbleton, asking for some background information for a book he was researching about another country house – and we were pleased to help. One thing led to another and we are now delighted to see the history of 'Dumbleton Hall' in his capable hands, as yet another record of local history.

Personally I am delighted that my amateur attempt to build an archive has been translated into this record by a personable gentleman, in every sense of the word, who has unselfishly thrown himself into this project, with a style I find readable and fascinating by its digressions and factual knowledge.

My own research led me on an interesting path; I had initially no idea of where to start. The Royal Agricultural College at Cirencester was helpful regarding the Hall's first owner Edward Holland. A very helpful reply to my letters from the Duchess of Devonshire led me to contacts with Joan Leigh Fermor, and then to Lord Monsell's grandson Michael Casey who so generously let me borrow so much material about this fascinating period of the Hall's second ownership history. I was able to share much with the Dumbleton Society thanks to Don Caisey, placing fascinating material into a wider domain. I have tried to give John an outline of the Fellowship of Remembrance stewardship since 1959, but there are so many Fellowship members who have contributed so much over the years, who also make this story possible. The transition from a Members only facility to a fully commercial Hotel is another important change.

The 21st century has seen the hotel develop as a venue, under the highly professional management of General Manager Gavin Dron, who with Dexter Cairns has seen approaching 1,000 weddings and a wide variety of functions giving Dumbleton Hall the standing and visibility it deserves.

Behind all this still lies one important principle, or as POFR Chairman Alan Bealby calls it our 'raison d' etre'. The Fellowship was set up as a unique remembrance organisation and the 'Books of Remembrance' which we hold in trust are documents of national significance and are also part of the Dumbleton Story. Now read on......

Martin Grafton – Dumbleton Hall 2015

Dumbleton Hall – Timeline 'The First Thousand Years'

866 – *Earliest reference to Dumbleton. Ethelred I, brother of Alfred the Great, gives land at Dumbleton to Abingdon Abbey.*

1086 - *Dumbleton recorded in the Doomsday Book: 'Seven hides and a half (900 acres) – 4 plough tillages, 13 labourers, 8 small holders with 8 ploughs, 6 slaves, a mill valued at 6 shillings.'*

1287 – *Abbot of Abingdon claims free warren (i.e. rabbits) at Dumbleton. Robert of Mortimer holds the Manor of Dumbleton.*

1390 – *A yearly pension from 8d from the Church of Dumbleton for sick brethren in the Diocese of Worcester.*

1460 – *The* Daston *family builds the North Transept of Dumbleton Church.*

1538 – Abington Abbey was surrendered to the King on 9th February 1538

1543 – Dumbleton is acquired by Lord Audley and Sir Thomas Pope for £ 82 . 13 . 2d

1545 - Sir Thomas Pope becomes the sole owner and holds the Manor of Dumbleton for the next 20 years.

1559 – On Sir Thomas's death the *estate transfers to Pope's nephew, Edmund Hutchins who marries Dorothy, daughter of Thomas Cocks of Cleeve.*

1602 – *Edmund Hutchins dies, the estate is transferred to the Cocks family.*

1602 – *Dorothy Cocks marries Charles Percy, younger son of the Earl of Northumberland. Charles dies in 1628 & Dorothy in 1646 – no surviving children.*

1646 – *Dorothy's brother Charles Cocks holds the Manor of Dumbleton.*

1654 – Charles Cocks *dies and his son Richard Cocks succeeds him. He is created a Baronet in* 1663.

1665 – *Sir Richard Cocks is created High Sheriff of the County.*

1684 – *Sir Richard dies and his estate passes to his grandson, another Richard.*

c1690 – First Dumbleton Hall built – the site is today marked with an illustrated panel at the lower end of the drive and west of the Church. Sir Richard Cocks, like his grandfather, becomes High Sheriff and Knight of the Shire in three successive Parliaments.

1723 – Sir Richard's wife Frances dies.

1726 – Sir Richard Cocks dies and is succeeded by his nephew, another Robert.

1740 – Sir Robert dies and is succeeded by his son, another Robert.

1749 – Sir Robert's wife Elizabeth dies on the 30th January, along with – in a seventeen day period, three of their children, aged 3, 8, and 16.

1765 – Sir Robert Cocks dies from a fall from his horse and the estate passes to his sister Dorothy.

1767 – Dorothy Cocks dies

1767-1822 – The Estate is held by the Cocks's cousins, the Somers-Cockses of Castleditch (later renamed Eastnor, near Ledbury). Dumbleton is partially demolished and becomes a farm.

1822/3 – The Estate is sold to Swinton Colthurst Holland. The proceeds are used by the Somers-Cockses to pay off the building of Eastnor Castle.

1830– Edward Holland commissions the new Dumbleton Hall. The architect is G.S. Repton, son of the landscape gardener Humphrey Repton.

1832 – G.S. Repton, completes his commission.

1835 – Edward Holland becomes MP for East Worcestershire – 1835-37 & 1855-68. Twice married and father of 14 children all raised at Dumbleton Hall.

1850s – Visitors to Dumbleton include Mrs Gaskell, the novelist (her daughter Marianne marries Edward's eldest son Edward Thurston). Correspondence with Edward Holland included Charles Dickens and Charles Darwin.

1875 – Edward Holland dies and his son Thurston sells the Hall and the Estate for £180,000 to the Eyres family, whose wealth had been built up by the Yorkshire wool merchant Samuel Eyres.

1880 – Henry William Eyres of Dumbleton marries Caroline Isabel Sharp on the 20ᵗʰ October. He dies while on a visit to Naples a year later.

1904 – Eyres' daughter Sybil marries Bolton Monsell, who takes the name of Eyres-Monsell.

1905 – Dumbleton Hall is extended to the present size when the North wing was added at this time along with the porte cochere, the lodge and the gates. Much internal work was also carried out to the Mansion.

1910 – Bolton Eyres- Monsell becomes MP for Evesham. He holds this seat until his peerage in 1935.

1914 – He returns to the Navy for active service. He is mentioned in despatches and awarded the Order of the Nile for services in Egypt.

1923 – Eyres-Monsell appointed Privy Councillor and Chief Whip from 1923-31.

1920s & 30s– Dumbleton Hall's heyday as a country house with society parties, shooting, swimming, dances and tennis. Guests included John Betjeman, Diana Mitford and the only Mitford brother, Tom.

1931- Sir Bolton Eyres-Monsell becomes the First Lord of the Admiralty, a post he held until 1936.

1936 – Bolton Eyres-Monsell becomes Viscount Lord Eyres-Monsell of Evesham.

1941 – Lord Eyres-Monsell serves as a regional Commissioner for Civil Defence in the south-west region of England until 1945.

1940s – The Women's Land Army are billeted on the top floor of Dumbleton Hall.

1946 – Lord Eyres-Monsell's only son Graham is awarded the Medal of Freedom Bronze Palm by the US Congress for intelligence work in North America and Italy.

1950 – Lord and Lady Monsell divorce – Lord Monsell marries the granddaughter of Field Marshall John French, Earl of Ypres.

1959 – Dumbleton Hall is sold by Lady Monsell (separate from the Estate) for £180,000 to the Post Office Fellowship of Remembrance. Had a buyer at the time not been found, the Hall was proposed to have been demolished.

1960 – The Hall, with a Matron and Manager, opens to provide holiday facilities for Post Office employees. It was funded as a living memorial to those men and women of the post office who had died in the First and Second World Wars. A memorial garden was laid out in the former swimming pool area and books of remembrance kept at the Hall.

1970s – A bar is installed and the larger bedrooms divided and en-suites added to modernise the Hall.

1996 – In October 1996 The Dumbleton Hall Hotel opens its doors for the first time to the general public and the hotel starts to offer function facilities for weddings and conferences.

2000s – A rolling programme is in place to upgrade all the bedrooms and the function areas of the hotel to bring it in line with other local hotels and to specialise in fine weddings and take advantage of the Hall itself and the magnificent gardens.

(Thanks to Mr Martin Grafton for the time and patience in compiling this timeline of Dumbleton and to Mr Adrian Phillips for any corrections)

* *

Colour Plates

1. 1st Earl Somers –Romney:-courtesy of the Eastnor Castle Collection©
2. Edward Holland:-courtesy of the 'University of Agriculture,' Cirencester©
3. The Gold Medals Awarded for the best Student who gained the Diploma in Estate Management:- courtesy of Lorna Parker (archivist) & the 'University of Agriculture' in Cirencester©
4. The OS Map of Dumbleton Hall for 1883:- courtesy of OS and to Sue Campbell©
5. Mrs Eyres at Dumbleton c1900 before the building of the 'porte-cochere: - courtesy of the Dumbleton Society & the late Don Caisey©
6. Chatsworth House – Derbyshire
7. Charles Darwin as a child
8. Early Sketch of Dumbleton Hall:- courtesy of the 'Dumbleton Society' & the late Don Caisey©
9. Dumbleton Hall in August 2014:- courtesy of JRH©
10. Dumbleton Hall from the west- showing the original house and the later north extension in summer 2014:-JRH©
11. Dumbleton facing west with the more formal gardens in c1923/4:-courtesy of Mr Martin Grafton-Archivist©
12. Dumbleton Hall in the Snow: courtesy of Matt Davis-Photographer©
13. Kathleen Mary Ferrier 1912-1953 & the Memorial piano at Dumbleton Hall
14. Kathleen Ferrier travelled to sing in New York on board the 'Queen Mary' the 'Queen Elizabeth' and the 'R.M.S. Mauretania'
15. A Women's Land Army Poster from World War 2- Dumbleton was a Land Girl Hostel from 1943 to 1947
16. Early view of the Hall and the gardens in their heyday:-courtesy of the Dumbleton Society & the late Don Caisey©
17. Early photograph of the Drawing Room at Dumbleton Hall:-courtesy of the Dumbleton Society and the late Don Caisey©
18. Patrick and Joan Fermor's Greek home at Kalamitsi in 2014
19. Bolton Meredith Eyres-Monsell, 1st Viscount Monsell, GBE, PC – 1881-1969:-courtesy of the National Portrait Gallery, London ©
20. The dining room made ready for a wedding:- courtesy of Mr Martin Grafton, Mr. Simon Kelly, the manager Mr Gavin Dron and the Dumbleton Hotel©
21. Friar's Carse in Scotland and Waterhead in the Lake District another of the Post Office Fellowship of Remembrance Homes: courtesy of Mr Martin Grafton©
22. The Monsell Memorial Window in St Olave's Church, Hart Street, London:-Photograph by Phil Manning Image© St Olave Church, Hart Street, London PCC 2015 by permission.
23. Dumbleton Hall in the spring:-courtesy of Mr Simon Kelly and the Dumbleton Hall Hotel©

* *

Chapter One: The Early History of Dumbleton

Dumbleton lies on the north side of one of the hills which is an outlier of the Cotswold edge, and close to the famous Bredon Hill. The ending of the name 'ton' indicates the village of Dumbleton had Saxon origins. 'The English Place Name Society' has suggested that the name means 'leafy dell or a brambly place.' The origins of the village may be older still and derive not from the Anglo Saxon 'dun' (a down) but from the Goidhelic Celtic 'dun' or 'dum' (a fortress). We do not know for certain but Dumbleton's origins are certainly to be found in the far distant past.

The earliest reference to Dumbleton was through Ethelred I, who was the brother of Alfred the Great, who is noted for giving lands at Dumbleton to Abingdon Abbey in 866. Ethelred was also written as 'Aethelred' in most documents.

An early coin from the time of Aethelred

King Aethelred I was born in c837 and died in 871. He is in fact related to the present queen of England being her 32nd great- granduncle.

He married Wulfrida and had two sons. He was buried at Wimbourne after dying of the wounds he had received at Witchampton in Hampshire. He was succeeded by his brother Alfred the Great. His reign was a difficult and violent one, with continual struggles against the Danish invaders under Ivar the Boneless and his brother Halfdan.

In connection with Dumbleton, and the Abbey of Abingdon, we learn a little about an early foundation. It has been suggested that a monastery dedicated to St Mary and a nunnery dedicated to St Helen were established here at Abingdon by a brother and sister, Hean and Cilla, in the 7th Century and the Abingdon Chronicles have stated that the ancient building of this first abbey was mostly in ruins by the time that Aethelwold arrived from Glastonbury in AD 953 to refound it. He obviously had some interest in the foundation having given land to the abbey at Dumbleton.

After the Norman Conquest in 1066, William the Conqueror ordered the Domesday Book to record his new kingdom and in 1086 we find that Dumbleton was recorded at this time as having: '*Seven hides and a half (about 900 acres) - 4 ploughs, 13 labourers, 8 small holders with 8 ploughs, 6 slaves and a mill valued at 6 shillings' (Today: In 1270, £0 6s 0d would have the same spending worth as 2005's £159.82).*

The lands of Dumbleton must have still belonged to the much extended and richer Abbey of Abington in 1287 when it is mentioned that the Abbot of Abington claimed free warrens (a free collection of rabbits) at Dumbleton. At this time the manor was held by Robert of Mortimer.

Robert de Mortimer, of Richards Castle was only 22 at the time of his father's death. He had livery of his inheritance in December 1274. In 1277 he was summoned for military service in Wales where he performed well (for 3 knight's fees) with five servants including William and Hugh de Mortimer. He was summoned again in person in 1282 and 1283.

After the death of Roger de Mortimer of Wigmore, Robert, as one of the Lords Marchers, was directed to put himself under the orders of Roger Lestrange. He is said to have been one of those who slew Llewelyn, Prince of Wales, in a chance encounter at Builth in December 1282. In June 1283 he was summoned to the assembly at Shrewsbury, and in the same year, in reward for his good service in the expedition to Wales, his debts to the Crown were remitted. He had licence to hunt the fox, hare, badger and cat in the forests of Essex. He married Joyce, daughter and heir of William de la Zouch, who had Norton in Northants and other manors. He died 7 April 1287, and was buried next day in Worcester Cathedral, before the altar of Saints Simon and Jude. Dower was assigned to his widow Joyce in November 1287. She was buried near him, 13 March 1289/90.

The connection must have continued with Worcester Cathedral or at least with the diocese as in 1390 it was recorded that '*a yearly pension from 8d from the church at Dumbleton for the sick in the Diocese of Worcester.'*

The next mention of Dumbleton to be discovered in historic records was in 1460 when the Daston Family built the north transept of Dumbleton Church.

At the time of the Dissolution of the Monasteries, when Abingdon was dissolved, the land at Dumbleton went to Sir Thomas Pope, who is then recorded as holding the Manor of Dumbleton for 20 years. Sir Thomas is an interesting character of his time and worthy of a mention in this text, even though he probably never actually came to Dumbleton, except perhaps to hunt or collect his tax dues.

Sir Thomas Pope (c1507 – 29 January 1559), founder of Trinity College, Oxford was born at Deddington, near Banbury, Oxfordshire, probably in 1507, for he was about sixteen years old when his father, a yeoman farmer, died in 1523.

Sir Thomas Pope by John Faber Sr:- courtesy of the National Portrait Gallery©

He was educated at Banbury School and Eton College, and entered the Court of Chancery. He there found a friend and patron in the Lord Chancellor Thomas Audley. As Clerk of Briefs in the Star Chamber, Warden of the Mint (1534–1536), Clerk of the Crown in Chancery (1537), and second officer and treasurer of the Court of Augmentations for the settlement of the confiscated property of the smaller religious foundations, he obtained immense wealth and influence. In this last office he was superseded in 1541, but from 1547 to 1553 he was again employed as fourth officer. He himself won by grant or purchases a considerable share in the spoils of the Dissolution, for nearly 30 manors, which came sooner or later into his possession, and were originally church property. "*He could have rode,*" said Aubrey, "*in his owne lands from Cogges (by Witney) to Banbury, about 18 miles.*" He established his country seat at Tittenhanger, Hertfordshire.

COLLEGIVM TRINITATIS,

Trinity College, Oxford in 1566 shortly after its foundation-original engraving lost by John Bereblock (fl.1557-1572)

Trinity College was founded in 1555 by Sir Thomas Pope, and the college was built on land bought after the abolition of Durham College, of which a small part including the library still exists today.

The library or what remains of Durham College, Oxford today

Durham was abolished during the Reformation and although Pope was a Catholic, he wanted to found a College whose students could say prayers for his soul, and his body is, in fact buried beside the present altar in the College chapel. He had no surviving children and so he hoped to be remembered by the students of his new college.

The original foundation made provision for a president, 12 fellows and 12 scholars, and up to 20 undergraduates. The fellows were required to take Holy Orders and to remain unmarried.

The College remained largely an all-male institution until 1979 when (in common with a number of other Oxford colleges) it admitted its first women undergraduates. It is today fully co-educational and co-residential.

Eton College in 1690-engraving by David Loggan

The Manor of Dumbleton was held by Pope for over 20 years, but passed in 1558 to Thomas's nephew Edmund Hutchins who married Dorothy who was the daughter of Thomas Cocks of Cleeve.

According to the College records we have the following written about Thomas Cocks and his connection with Dumbleton.

'Born in Oxfordshire. the founder's nephew, and one of his heirs'. Admitted scholar of Trin coll. Oxon. Octob, 3, 1556, by the founders mandate', Page 419 Aet. 22. He quitted the college about Christmas 1558'. He lived at

5

Dumbleton in Gloucestershire, where he was Lord of the Manor, and married the Daughter of Thomas Cockes, esquire. By his will, dat Jan. 28. 44 Eliz. and proved soon afterwards, he left to Trinity college aforesaid the advowson to the church of Dumbleton. Also estates, worth per ann. 33l. 6s. 8d. part of which the said college was annually to pay to certain charitable uses, and to have the residue. But his coheirs claiming the pre/misses, the whole benefaction was set aside by a de/cree of chancery. He left besides, other charitable bequests to places with which he was connected. He was a benefactor to the library, in 1592. On a but/tress, on the south side of the college, the following memorial of him remains, cut in the stone.

"Jesu have M. O. E. HUTCHINS."

1558. i. e. Jesus have mercy on Edmund Hutchins.'

On the death of Edmund in 1602 the Dumbleton estate passes to the Cocks family whose connection with Dumbleton would last for over 200 years. Dorothy inherits the estate and in this same year Dorothy Cocks marries Charles Percy, the younger son of the Earl of Northumberland. Charles died in 1628 and Dorothy in 1646. The couple left no surviving children.

*'**Charles**, fourth son, knighted in France, by Robert Earl of Essex, anno 1591; married Dorothy, daughter of Richard **Cox**, of **Dumbleton** in Com. Gloucester. Esq.'*

There is an interesting tomb in the Church at Dumbleton which gives us an idea of what the couple looked like and their sadness at the loss of their child.

Sir Charles Percy was a follower of the young Earl of Essex, a favourite of Queen Elizabeth I. He went with him on a successful expedition to Normandy to help Henry IV. In 1598, Percy went to Ireland while Essex was Lord-Lieutenant. Instead of subduing a rebellion by the Earl of Tyrone, he made peace with him. Essex and Percy were thrown into the Tower of London. Essex was beheaded, but Sir Charles was released.

In 1603, he took news of the Queen's death to James I in Edinburgh. He retired to Dumbleton, and married Dorothy, widow of the late Squire Edmund Hutchings. He may have found life dull at times, for he asked Mr. Carlington to send news of the happenings in London. He wished not to be taken for Justice Silence or Justice Shallow — two characters from Shakespeare's "The Merry Wives of Windsor" —

Charles and Dorothy Percy in Dumbleton Church:-JRH©

Mr Adrian Phillips (with help from Dr Caroline Barron, who deciphered the wills of Dorothy Cocks and others) has kindly allowed me to use his notes concerning Dorothy Cocks who had such a profound influence on the history of Dumbleton. It has been assumed that the Percys lived in the village, but on reading her will which had been proven on the 28th January 1648 (at the height of the English Civil war), Dorothy asks that her body be buried in the Church at Dumbleton, with that of her daughter (but strangely there is no reference to her being buried with the body of her late husband. The will also refers to the arrangements that are to be made for the 'Manor House of Dumbleton' and for the servants who lived there. It is fairly clear that she lived in this manor in the village. Since there was not a manor house in Hutchins's time, it is reasonable to assume that the Percys had their own house somewhere in Dumbleton. Dorothy lived here alone for 18 years of her life. The mystery lies as to where this manor house must have been and there are two possibilities. Possibly to the west of the Church, on the same site that Sir Richard Cocks built his own fine mansion in c1695, or could it have been where the 'Old Rectory' stands

8

today? If this is so, the southern half-timbered part of the present house (as well as the cellar under the north section) are the remains of what was the Percy's Manor house. If the first explanation is correct, Sir Richard must have wholly demolished the old family home to build his new mansion; if however, the second explanation is correct, then he partially rebuilt the family home as a rectory for his younger brother.

To complicate matters further, Edmund Hutchins left money to Trinity College as already mentioned and required that they appoint a resident rector in the village. In the understanding therefore, of where the manor house may have been, one also has to explain where the rectory originally was. The Terrier (land records) of 1666 and 1668 make no mention of a rectory, although the 1668 terrier does state that: *'Ye Parson' had a house, garden, orchard and 52 acres of land.'*

So we have an enigma still to solve concerning the rectory and the Percy's manor house, but we do know that Dorothy and her second husband made the village their home, employed a wide range of servants and workers and helped to transform Dumbleton into the fine estate village that it became under her great-nephew, Sir Richard Cocks.

It is also interesting to note the connection between Charles and Jocelyn Percy (younger brothers of the Earl of Northumberland) and the Earl of Essex, as they paid for a performance of Richard II at the 'Globe Theatre' on the eve of their armed rebellion against Queen Elizabeth. This gives us a connection between Dumbleton and William Shakespeare.

Shakespeare's 'Chamberlain's Men' do not appear to have suffered from their association with the Essex group; but they were commanded to perform it for the Queen on Shrove Tuesday in 1601, the day before Essex's execution. She knew the Percys favoured Essex, but, then, so had she – once.

* *

Dorothy's brother Charles Cocks holds the Manor of Dumbleton until his death, when the Manor passes to his son.

Sir Richard Cocks was created a Baronet in 1663. In 1665 Sir Richard becomes the High Sheriff of the County. He died in 1684 and the Dumbleton estate passes to his grandson, also named Richard.

'b. c.1659, 1st s. of Richard Cocks of the Middle Temple, (d.v.p. o. s. of Sir Richard Cocks, 1st Bt., of Dumbleton), by Mary, da. of Sir Robert Cooke⁺ of Highnam, Glos., and sis. of William Cooke I*. educ. M. Temple 1667; Oriel, Oxf. 1677-by 1680. m. (1) lic. 6 Oct. 1688, Frances (d. 1724), da. of Richard Neville*, s.p.; (2) by Nov. 1724, Mary (d.

1764), da. of William Bethell of Swindon, Yorks., s.p. suc. fa. 1669; gdfa. as 2nd Bt. 16 Sept.'   1684.

Sir Richard became Sheriff of Gloucestershire from 1692-3 and Freeman of Evesham by 1697.

The following biography gives an interesting outline of Richard's career

'Tradition, upheld by the Member himself, located the common origin of the Cocks family in Kent, but the Gloucestershire branch can be traced back no farther than the mid-16th century, to a Thomas Cocks of Bishop's Cleeve. The manor of Dumbleton was acquired through marriage by Thomas Cocks's daughter, from whom it passed in two removes to the 1st baronet, a staunch adherent of King Charles I and 'a great sufferer for his love to the royal family and for his zeal for the laws and established religion of his country'. This cavalier heritage meant little to the 2nd baronet, his grandson, who took the path of Whiggery, perhaps influenced by his wife's family or even by his cousin Charles Cocks*, a brother-in-law of Lord Somers (Sir John*). In other respects too, the succession of the 2nd baronet marked a new departure: he was responsible for the rebuilding of Dumbleton, which he had returned to occupy after the death of his grandmother in 1690; and his ambitions to play a part in local and national politics were soon realized. He was involved in the manoeuvring that preceded the county election in 1690, at first active in support of Sir John Guise, 2nd Bt.*, and later making promises of goodwill, perhaps genuine, to Lord Weymouth's brother James Thynne*. Sheriff in 1692, and chairman of the Gloucestershire quarter sessions from at least 1696, he stood unsuccessfully against Sir Francis Winnington* in the neighbouring borough of Tewkesbury in 1695, and at the next election was returned as knight of the shire on the Whig interest, receiving a sour tribute from one opponent, who dubbed him 'an ill-favoured orator of that county'.2

Cocks's parliamentary career is unusually well documented, thanks to the survival of his memoranda-books. Beginning as a record of some of his own letters and speeches (prepared if not always delivered), his views on matters of theology, morality and politics, and interesting facts culled from the Votes and from papers laid before the House, these notes extended into a parliamentary diary comparable in length to that of Narcissus Luttrell*, though much more vivid and personal, covering parts of the sessions of 1698–9 and 1699–1700, and forming a near-continuous record of proceedings in these years.

In his last years Cocks became even more determinedly eccentric. When his wife died in 1724 he erected a monument on which was inscribed his gratitude for the years she had lived 'in peace, harmony and tranquillity with her husband, as far as human imbecilities common to the best of mortals would permit'. He immediately remarried, and in a new will gave his second wife a life interest in his estate. His last pamphlet, published posthumously, purported to be an inquiry into the so-called 'bloody execution' at Thorn, together with 'a vindication of some of the tenets of the Quakers', but was in fact nothing more than a stale reprise of past polemics against popery and High Church priestcraft, the flavour of which is conveyed by his description of Anglican ordination:

We often see an ignorant, immoral dunce, because he was a relation of the bishop's or his wife's, or for marrying a poor relation or an old servant maid, or sometimes without that drudgery, by making a present to the wife or steward, it will open a way, and prevail upon an old, doting fellow to lay his hands on him, and by that means imprint on him an indelible character, and give him credentials to be from thenceforth an ambassador of Heaven.

After spending some time at Bath in 1726, afflicted by the gout, he died about 21 Oct. of that year, and was buried at Dumbleton. Predictably, in the preamble to his will he gave vent to his natural self-opinionated verbosity, on the worthlessness of deathbed repentances. Under the terms of the will, which took some 11 years to prove, the estate passed directly to a nephew and on his death without issue in 1765, to a kinsman from Herefordshire, who demolished the greater part of the house. The baronetcy had already become extinct. 8'

(Unless otherwise stated, this biography is based on the evidence of Cocks's own diary and commonplace books (Bodl. mss Eng. hist. b. 209-10, published as The Parliamentary Diary of Sir Richard Cocks, 1698-1702 ed. D. W. Hayton).

It was in the 1690s that the first **Dumbleton Hall** was built. The site being shown at the lower end of the drive, west of the church and dealt with in detail in the following chapter.

In 1740 the next Sir Robert Cocks inherits the Dumbleton estate. In 1749 his wife Elizabeth dies on the 30th January and within a 17 day period three of their children aged 3, 8 and 16 also died. In 1765 just 16 years later Sir Robert dies from a fall from his horse. The tragedy of the family is inscribed on his memorial plaque in the Church.

In Memory of Sir Robert Cocks Bar.! who after fustaining with Chriftian fortitude and refignation the moft Affecting Lofs of an Amiable wife and three Children in the Courfe of a few Days by a Cruel Diftemper which Attaked his Family, had the Misfortune to Loofe his own Life by a fall from his Horfe in April 1765 and lies Buried near this place.

The memorial to Sir Robert Cocks Bt in Dumbleton Church;JRH©

In 1767 Dorothy Cocks, Sir Robert's only surviving child dies and the Dumbleton estate was then held by the Cocks's cousins, the Somers-Cockses of Castleditch, later Eastnor near Ledbury.

Eastnor Castle: courtesy of the Eastnor Castle Collection©

Between 1767 and 1822 the Dumbleton Estate was owned by the Cocks's cousins, the Somers – Cockses of Castleditch, later Eastnor near Ledbury. The Old Dumbleton Hall was partially demolished and became a farm.

Eastnor was built by the 2nd Baron between 1810 and 1824, and it is therefore probable that the sale of the Dumbleton estate in 1822 helped to meet the bills.

* *

The 1st Earl Somers (6th May 1760 – 5th January 1841) was known as the Lord Somers between 1806 and 1821. He was a British peer and a politician of note.

The 1st Earl Somers-Romney:-courtesy of the Eastnor Castle Collection© (see colour plate)

Somers was the son of Charles Cocks, who was 1st Baron Somers and Elizabeth, who was the daughter of Richard Eliot. He was educated at Westminster School and later at St Alban's Hall in Oxford.

St Alban's Hall – Oxford, today part of Merton College – by F. Mackenzie & J. le Keux
c1836

Early picture of Westminster School after Pugin

After completing his studies he became a Member of Parliament for West Looe in Cornwall in 1784 and 1790 and finally he served for Reigate between 1790 and 1806. In the later years of his career he became a member of the House of Lords and in 1817 became Lord Lieutenant of Herefordshire, a post which he held until his death in 1841.

In 1821, a year before the sale of Dumbleton, he was created Viscount Eastnor, of Eastnor Castle near Ledbury and Herefordshire and Earl Somers.

Lord Somers married twice, firstly in 1785 to Margaret who was the daughter of the Reverend Tradway, Russell Nash. Through the marriage they had three sons and one daughter. His eldest son, Edward Charles Cocks, who was a British Army officer, was killed in March 1812 at the Siege of Burgos during the Peninsular War.

The 1ˢᵗ Earl Somers later in life by John Harrison Jnr:-courtesy of the Eastnor Castle Collection©

After the loss of his first wife in February 1831, Lord Somers married three years later in 1834, his first cousin, Jane, daughter of James Cocks and widow of the Reverend George Waddington. There were no children born to this marriage and Lord Somers died in the January of 1841 aged 80 years. He was succeeded in his titles by his second, but his eldest surviving son, John. His wife the Countess died in the November of 1868.

In connection with **Dumbleton**, the estate had been sold by Lord Somers in 1822, with the proceeds going towards building Eastnor Castle at Ledbury and this ended the connection with Dumbleton.

Dumbleton Estate was bought by Sir Swinton Holland in c1822, although there is little evidence to suggest he actually lived at Dumbleton. There are various references to his estate such as:

'Deputation to Thomas Pallat to act as a gamekeeper of Dumbleton & Cockbury by Swinton Colthurst Holland Esq. Lord of the Manor made 24th August 1824 – Registered at Quarter Sessions 27th August 1824).' A similar deputation to a Benjamin Harris to act as a gamekeeper for the Dumbleton & Cockbury estates by Swinton Colthurst Holland was dated 25th July 1826 and registered at the Quarter Sessions on the 15th August 1826.

There is also the collection of Mrs Gaskell material housed at the Brotherton Library at the University of Leeds which contains *'Particulars of the Dumbleton Estate'* and was printed in 1822.

Colthurst Holland died in 1827 on a visit to Naples, leaving a pregnant wife and the estate to his son Edward, who lived here until his death in 1875. Swinton and his wife's monument can be found in the Church. She died in 1845.

In 1830 Edward Holland commissions a new Dumbleton Hall, buying fully the estate for £80,000 (In 1830, £18,000 0s 0d would have the same spending worth of 2005's £890,820.00)

(Reference: G. E. C., ed. Geoffrey F. White. *The Complete Peerage*. (London: St. Catherine Press, 1953) Vol. XII, Part 1, p. 32.)

* *

Chapter Two: The First Dumbleton Hall

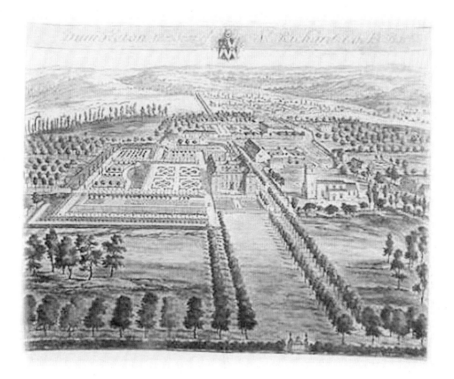

Copper engraving, '**Dumbleton, the Seat of Sir. Richard Cocks Bart.**', from Britannia Illustrata, or Views of Several of the Queens Palaces also of the Principal Seats of the Nobility and Gentry of Great Britain (London, 1709)

There is today nothing left of the first Dumbleton Hall built for *Sir Richard Cocks* in 1690.

The present day undulations in the grounds just inside the main entrance to the present Hall give some impression of the garden layout shown in the Kip engraving that was published in 1712. There are today a couple of large trees growing on the site.

The gardens for Richard Cocks are said to be similar in layout and detail to those found today at *Westbury Court* near Westbury-on-Severn. Here are some examples of what the first Dumbleton Hall gardens may have looked like:

In 1707, a bird's-eye view of Westbury Court and its garden was engraved by Johannes Kip for his *Britannia Illustrata:*

The gardens today at Westbury Court:-courtesy of the National Trust and Ann Davies the Business Support Officer©

Westbury Court:-courtesy of the National Trust & Ann Davies the Business Support Officer©

The sketch plan given by J. C. L. Ellis-Marshall in the first edition of a pamphlet *Lands called Dumbleton* is probably a misinterpretation of the Kip engraving, which was partially confirmed by a resistivity survey.

We can see clearly, that the 1822 sale map shows a north-south arm of the canal between the D-shaped pool and the house up to the northern canal. Though this feature is omitted from both the Kip engraving, and the Ellis-Marshall sketch, it probably existed in 1712. Thus Kip's engraving cannot be relied upon, and probably exaggerated the extent of the garden.

Westbury Court Garden at Westbury–on-Severn, Gloucestershire is a Dutch water garden in the style of what was once thought to have existed at Dumbleton Old Hall. It was laid out between 1696 and 1705 and is a rare survival. It was not replaced by later styles and fashions such as the naturalistic garden landscape popularised by Capability Brown, which is more the style for the new Dumbleton Hall commissioned later by Edward Holland.

The gardens at Westbury were created by the then owner of Westbury Court, *Maynard Colchester I*, between 1697, when the brook was first diverted, and in 1705.

The idea for the creation of the gardens may have come from the canal garden of nearby *Flaxley Abbey*, which was the seat of Maynard's close friend *Catharina Boevey*, who was the widow of William Boevey, a member of a Dutch merchant family who had settled in London. The Kip engraving of Flaxley shows a long rectangular canal, of which only faint traces exist today. Clipped accents to set off the pyramidal yews were provided by 'headed' Laurustinus, headed and pyramidal Phillyrea and Mizerean trees in sixes and in pairs.

Flaxley Abbey from an engraving by Johannes Kip in 1712

As can be seen in the above engraving, the centrepiece of the gardens is a 137 meters long canal centred on a two storey Dutch style red brick pavilion at one end and a wrought iron gate in the wall at the far end, designed to extend the vista from the pavilion on into the surrounding countryside. The canal is flanked by yew and holly topiary in the shape of pyramids and balls.

A second red brick building, a summer house was built in 1702-4 overlooking a T-shaped canal running parallel with the main canal. Behind the summer house is a small walled garden of cottage plants and beyond the water garden is an orchard of fruit trees, which contains an ancient evergreen oak planted in the 17th century, the largest ever recorded. It is claimed to be one of the oldest surviving evergreen oaks in England.

The canal at Westbury Court c1902©

In 1712 Dumbleton Old Hall is across a carriage drive from the church. Its south front faces a park between twin tree avenues, of which no vestige remains. These were either felled or fell to disease or just old age and no longer exist.

The western elevation of the Old Hall fronts a parterre with raised terraced walks about one metre above the parterres surrounding it. The furthest cross-raised terrace was an alley with a bower at its northern end. This idea can be shown in the photograph from Westbury Court.

The channel that fed the water supply is visible. The 1822 sale map indicates a pool about SP01253541, which may have been involved with this.

There is a central path that leads to a D-shaped pool with a statue making an ornamental fountain. It was likely to have been gravity-fed using springs on Dumbleton Hill. It then flows under the raised terrace walk on the north side to a canal that linked to another canal along the northern side of the garden. At its eastern end it widens to provide a farmyard pool close to the stables. These are marked as fish pools on the schedule associated with the 1822 sale plan.

On the western side of the pool was a dovecote.

The site of a circular pool where once the gardens of the Old Hall were placed:-JRH

24

The canal on the southern side of the garden appears to have been at a lower level. It lies alongside the potager below the southern raised walkway.

Beyond the western end of the garden Kip shows a plantation, whilst tree avenues line approaches from the south.

(Information researched with permission of the 'Park and Gardens UK Record' id:4208)

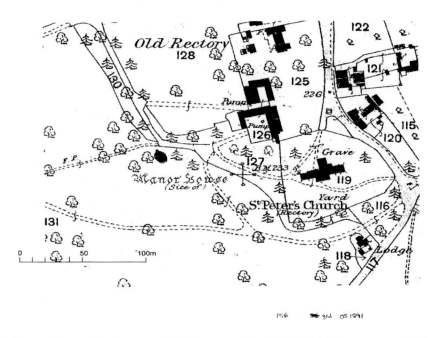

Ordnance Survey 6 inches per mile Gloucestershire XIII NW 1891: courtesy of OS and 'The Dumbleton Society' and the late Don Caisey©

Old Dumbleton Hall was built c1690 by Sir Richard Cocks (1659-1726). On his death, he was buried in the Church close by. He had no children so his nephew Sir Robert Cocks inherited the estate. The Estate and Hall in turn passed to his son, another Sir Robert in 1740.

The Hall built by Sir Richard must have been a very fine 17th Century mansion. This illustration taken from 'Lands Called Dumbleton' gives us an idea of what it may have looked like:

Old Dumbleton Hall:-courtesy of 'Lands Called Dumbleton' and given to me by The Dumbleton Society and the late Don Caisey©

Chapter Three: The Present Dumbleton Hall and Edward Holland

Swinton Colthurst Holland (1777-1827) who was a London Banker bought the Dumbleton Estate in 1822/3. His son Edward (1806-1875) inherited the estate and set about commissioning the new Dumbleton Hall.

Edward Holland MP President of the Royal Agricultural Society 1873-74- by Solomon Cole (19th Century)

In 1822 Earl Sommers put his manor of Dumbleton and the estate of nineteen hundred acres on the market. The church is early Norman and Early English in style and the rectory was enlarged in about 1700. It is a beautiful black and white timber and Stanway stone building. A good part of the village belonged to the estate apart from one of the farms which belonged to *Jesus College* in Oxford and a small property belonging to a Mr T. P. Staight. The estate and manor was advertised as being 'only 95 miles distant from London, very convenient for occupation' which in this era when transport was not easy, appears rather optimistic.

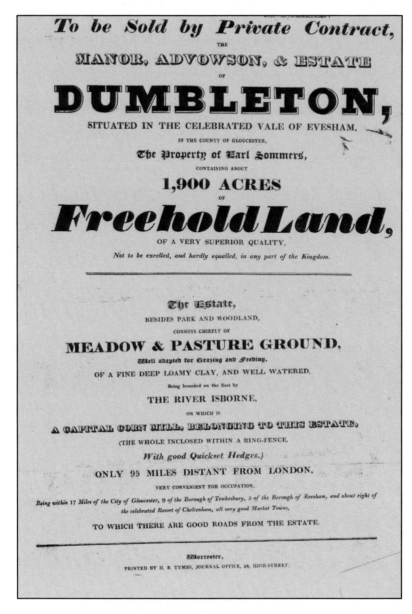

Sale Catalogue of the Sale by Lord Sommers of the Dumbleton Estate: courtesy of the Gloucester Archives©

In the June of 1822/3 Swinton Colthurst Holland bought or raised loans on the estate for eighteen thousand pounds. He had apparently paid for it by selling trust stock in English Fund to reinvest in New York State canal stock. He told Josiah Wedgwood (grandson of the famous potter), about this in a letter that talked about money, investments and the possibility of taxes on earth ware in the next budget, which would affect Josiah a great deal.

* *

Josiah Wedgwood III – 1795-1880 was a grandson of the famous English potter Josiah Wedgwood. He was a friend of Henry Holland. He was the eldest son of Josiah Wedgwood II and his wife Elizabeth Allen.

Josiah Wedgwood the first and his son Josiah Wedgwood II

In 1823 he was taken into partnership in the Wedgwood Pottery Company by his father and employed here until 1842 when he retired to Leith Hill in Surrey.

Josiah married his cousin Caroline Darwin (1800-1888), the daughter of Robert Darwin and sister to Charles Darwin whom Henry Holland also knew. They had four daughters, and his third daughter Margaret Susan Wedgwood (1843-1937), married The Reverend Arthur Vaughan Williams. Their son was the composer Ralph Vaughan Williams.

Charles Darwin and Ralph Vaughan Williams as young men

It was stated that on the 27th December 1827, Swinton had taken up his pen to sign a cheque in Mr Baring's counting house, fell back and died within minutes. Henry Holland in his journal stated that Swinton was only fifty years old, 'in perfect health, & abounding in all manner of worldly prosperity.' His son Edward inherited the estate:

Edward Holland (1806-1875), was a British Liberal Party politician from Worcestershire. He was elected as a Member of Parliament in the 1835 general election as member for East Worcestershire, but later defeated at the 1837 elections. He returned to the House of Commons after an 18 year absence, when he was elected at a by-election in July 1855 as the Member of Parliament for his local town, Evesham. He held this seat until he stepped down in the 1868 general election.

In the records for the 'Alumni Cantabrigienses', Cambridge University can be found the following biography for Edward:

'Holland, Edward. Adm. Pens. (age 18) at Trinity, Sept 29, 1823. S. of Swinton Colthurst (of Peover, Cheshire, and sometime of Roehampton, Surrey). B. (Feb 12 1806) in Trieste. School, Eton. Matric Michs. 1824; BA 1829; MA 1850. Adm. At Lincoln Inn, Jan 15, 1827. Married (1) 1832, Sophia (d.1851), dau. of Elias Isaac, of Boughton, Worcester, banker; (2) 1857, Frances Maria, dau. Of Samuel Christian, of Malta, and widow of J. Hunter, and had issue. Lord of the Manor znd patron of Dumbleton, Gloucs. J.P. and D.L for Gloucestershire and Worcester. High Sheriff of Worcs. 1842. MP for East Worcs., 1835-7; for Evesham 1855-68. Took a great interest in Agriculture, and prominently associated with the establishment of the Royal Agricultural College at Cirencester. President of the Royal Agricultural Society. Died Jan 4, 1875, aged 70. Father of Edward T. (1854) and Frederick W (1856); brother of George H. (1835).'*

A drawing of Edward Holland

30

Taking on his new inheritance, Edward decided that the Old Hall at Dumbleton was in such a ruinous state that he would create a model village and build himself a fine new mansion a little way from the present village and church for his family. He decided on the local honey coloured Cotswold stone and contacted *Humphrey Repton's* son *George* to design his new mansion in the currently fashionable *Tudor Gothic style*.

The contract for the new house was dated the 9th of January 1833 and the contract was annotated with a series of payments of £19,000 in total up to 9th September 1837. (Today this would have been equivalent to £940,310 making a total over the 4 years of £3,761,240). In 1832, the daughter of Charles Darwin, Catherine, wrote rather acidly 'It will be a nice house' after visiting Edward's mother, Mrs Anne Holland and her daughters Charlotte and Louisa, '*but Edward will be awfully pompous when he is master of it, for he can hardly contain his importance now.*' The new house is described as having first rate panelling and moulded plaster ceilings, probably the same one which exists in the entrance hall today. The especially fine staircase and large lantern are mentioned in early descriptions by Catherine. She mentions the large drawing room with its panoramic views over the surrounding countryside and the fine new 'Cedar of Lebanon' and 'Atlantic Cedar' trees. These still exist today and are magnificent in their mature state.

One of the splendid Cedar trees at Dumbleton planted by the Holland family when planning their new home and gardens:-JRH©

An ornamental lake is mentioned as part of the new design, although it was probably different to the present lake which was laid out later. Also mentioned in the early descriptions are the picturesque steep little hills in the parkland on which animals peacefully graze. Edward probably had a deer park enclosed in the front of the Hall.

The present views over the parkland and the ornamental lake in 2014:-JRH©

Edward ordered new carriage drives to be made through his parkland, which were entered through pattern-book lodges and gates which had been cut through the Old Hall's, Sir Richard Cocks's original garden. In 1832 the Holland family were living a few miles away at Overbury, which was a fine house rented from *Merton College.* This house was apparently crowded with pictures as Elizabeth Gaskell mentions to her friend Harriot Carr. These paintings were '*not always of the most delicate description'.*

Edward Holland: - courtesy of the Royal Agricultural University in Cirencester©(see colour plate)

The Elizabeth Gaskell mentioned was the famous '*Elizabeth Cleghorn Gaskell née Stevenson* – 1810-1865, often referred to as simply '*Mrs. Gaskell*'. She was a British novelist during the Victorian era. Her novels were popular in her day and even today as they give an insight into Victorian society. Elizabeth described in her novels not just the wealthy people but also the poor, which is of much interest to social historians.

Elizabeth Gaskell was a friend of the Bronte family and wrote the first biography on *Charlotte Bronte* which was published in 1857.

Charlotte Bronte and Elizabeth Gaskell

Mrs Gaskell was Edward Holland's cousin and her daughter Marianne married Edward's eldest son Thurston. Correspondence with Edward included letters from *Charles Dickens* and *Charles Darwin*, whose families he knew well. Edward, being an MP in one of the most interesting Victorian periods must have known and met many of the most notable people of the day. He was a truly fascinating character associated for so many years with Dumbleton Hall. It was a house he had created and where he had brought up his family and he obviously became very attached to the Hall and the spectacular countryside in this area of the Cotswolds.

Elizabeth Gaskell who was the cousin of Edward Holland in a portrait by George Richmond in 1851 and later in life

Edward Holland had an excellent education and had attended *Trinity College* in Cambridge in September 1823 and would have attended the college chapel and been obliged to make the Church of England subscription before taking his degree.

An early engraving of Trinity College-Cambridge

After leaving Cambridge he became a leading figure in the county and helped to found the *Royal Agriculture College at Cirencester* (today – the University College of Cirencester.). Edward became the MP for East Worcestershire in 1835-37 and again for Evesham from 1855-68.

A view of the Royal Agricultural College in 1860: courtesy of the Royal Agricultural University in Cirencester©

35

Edward became its first Chairman of the Council in 1845 and soon afterwards advanced thousands of pounds to ensure its continuance, when the college had financial problems and may have had to close. His role in the Royal Agricultural Society became also very influential. (Reference: The History of the Royal Agricultural College, Cirencester by Roger Sayce)

A view of the Royal Agricultural College in 1870:- courtesy of the Royal Agricultural University in Cirencester©

When Edward was at Cambridge he would have associated with families who were already famous in national life. He was a contemporary of *Hensleigh* and *Robert Wedgwood* (who later became the Rev Wedgwood and priest in charge at Dumbleton), and knew Charles Darwin's brother Erasmus well. Edward was, in fact, the second cousin of *Charles Darwin*.

Charles Darwin as a child and as a young man (see colour plate)

Edward Holland and his association with the Agricultural College at Cirencester- today the Royal Agricultural University of Cirencester- for reference I have used Roger Sayce's excellent book 'The History of the Royal Agricultural College - Cirencester' & I have been given permission and support from the Royal University of Agriculture & the archivist Lorna Parker. She has provided me with records and documentation for this chapter.

In 1842 a prospectus had been prepared and circulated with the view of obtaining patronage and support for a new agricultural college. Resolutions were passed, the principal one stating: *'That it is expedient to provide an Institution in which the rising generations of farmers, may receive instruction, at a moderate expense, in those sciences, a knowledge of which is essential to successful cultivation; and that is to form part of our institution.'* A committee was formed to implement the resolutions and Edward Holland was a member. Earl Bathurst was elected the President and Robert Jeffrey Brown became the Secretary.

In July 1844 there convened a *'General Meeting of Subscribers and Friends of the Proposed Agricultural College'* at Cirencester. At the meeting it was announced that Earl Bathurst had offered the site for the college and its farm. This was for a lease of forty-eight years of a farm of 430 acres near to Cirencester on the estate known as 'Port Farm.'

After several problems and the task of convincing other landowners of the importance of the new Agricultural College, sixty four members of the Council and the Chairman, Edward Holland were appointed; from this Council a committee was selected to draw up the by-laws and regulations for the College.

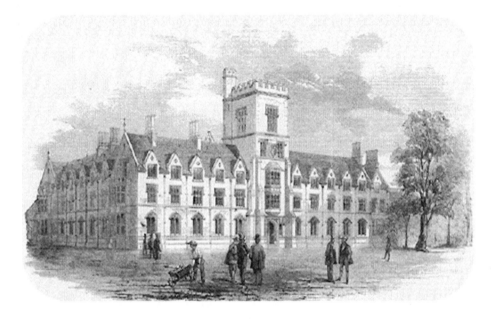

With the finances and the land thus assured the Council set about creating the College on the land leased from *Earl Bathurst*. They appointed as architects *Messrs Daukes and Hamilton of Gloucester and Cheltenham*, following a competition for the design of the College buildings. They were the winners from forty entries. The design utilized the existing farmhouse of *Port Farm* and the seventeenth-century tithe barn, but did not retain any of the other buildings of the farm.

In April 1847 the Chairman of the Council was *Edward Holland* who had taken over from *Raymond Cripps*. He was reporting the financial problems of the new College, and called for a general meeting of the shareholders to solve the liability problem of £8000 – to press those shareholders who were behind in their payments to pay their dues. A new issue of four hundred shares was also released in order to raise the necessary capital needed for the College to continue and hopefully grow. There was still much apathy in the general public and landowners needed to be convinced about the benefits of an agricultural college for their sons and their landowners and farmers.

John Corbett (1817-1901) who was the Worcestershire 'Salt King' and lived at *Impney Hall*, Droitwich in Worcestershire, had a large farming estate similar to Edward Holland. In fact, some of the land Impney had been built on, was purchased from the Somers-

Cocks family who preceded Edward Holland to the estate. John had tried to start his own Agricultural College but again due to lack of interest from other local landowners, John had to give up his plans. I am sure as an MP and a contemporary interested in agriculture and social reform the two men must have met and known of each other. (See John Hodges's book on *Chateau Impney* and *John Corbett volumes 1 & 2.*

* *

One of the recommendations from the meeting was to include the reduction of the number of staff in order to save costs and to open an office in London in order to show the College as a national rather than a local institution, and finally ensuring proper educational standards of students on entry.

It was at this time when the future of the new college appeared to be jeopardised that Edward Holland came to the rescue. He had been constant in his support of the College and its originator Robert Brown. When Edward came to report the Council accounts on 28th July 1847 the deficit was up to £10,800 and the College was in dire straits and facing extinction.

On the 5th August the Council received the following letter from him:

> '*Dumbleton, Evesham*
>
> *July 29th 1847*
>
> *Gentlemen,*
> *Unless the requisite funds are immediately found, you cannot receive back the pupils before Christmas, and the probability is, that if you remain closed until then you will lose those who are now ready to come to the College.*
>
> *Under the circumstances, I beg to state that I am willing to advance from time to time, between this and Christmas, such sums as may be necessary for the payment of pressing demands, upon the following conditions:*
> *1. That I have absolute control over both the College and the Farm.*
> *2. That all receipts, whether arising from the shares, donations, assets, Farm Sales or from any other source, shall from this date be passed to my credit, at one or other of the Cirencester Banks, as I may direct.*
> *3. That whenever such College and Farm Payments passed to my credit are sufficient amounts to balance my account, and that I am repaid all that I have advanced, together with all interest I may owe to the Bankers, then in such case the surplus, if any, is to be placed by me (to the credit of the College) in the hands of the Treasurers.*
>
> *I remain, Gentlemen,*
> *Faithfully Yours*
> *Edward Holland'*

This munificent offer was accepted without reservation by the Council: there was no other way out of the financial abyss. Later Edward Holland helped the College financially again to keep it stable and ongoing.

By the time of the Annual General Meeting of 1875 Edward had died. (He died this same year) and at this meeting the shareholders recorded their gratitude to him for his efforts on behalf of the College. This was certainly no more than his due and a Memorial Trust was set up to commemorate him and his munificence. The Records of this Trust were in the fires at the College in 1913 and 1923, but from the information later gained during the time of the Second World War, a gold medal was struck and is to this day awarded annually to the student who is first in order of merit on the *Estate Management* diploma course. It was one of two premier medals awarded to students. It was, in 1948, endowed by 3 1/2% War Stock to continue with the presentations that Edward had started.

The gold medal given by Edward Holland to award the first student in order of merit on the Estate Management Diploma:-courtesy of Lorna Parker (archivist) & the University College of Agriculture at Cirencester© (see colour plate)

An early photograph of the new college members' c1900

Life at Dumbleton Hall

The following Censuses for Dumbleton in 1841, 1851 and then again in 1861 make for some interesting reading and give us today an insight into who was living at the Hall in the Victorian period. Edward was married twice. His first wife is shown on the 1851 Census as *Sophia Holland* aged 35 and by 1861 he had lost his wife and was married again to *Francis Maria Holland* aged 36, so 19 years his junior. Edward had 14 children who were all brought up at Dumbleton.

Census for Dumbleton Hall 1841

Name	Age	Position	County Born	
Edward Holland	35	Head		No
Sophia Holland	35	Wife		No
Harriet S. Holland	6	Daughter	Dumbleton	Yes
Edward T. Holland	5	Son	Dumbleton	Yes
Frederick W. Holland	3	Son	Dumbleton	Yes
Caroline Holland	1	Daughter	Dumbleton	Yes
John Westover	45	Male Servant		No
William Dowdeswell	34	Male Servant		No
Anne Hinton	35	Female Servant		No
Charlotte Morris	40	Female Servant		No
Phebe Dickenson	35	Female Servant		No
Martha Lovell	25	Female Servant		No
Elizabeth Price	25	Female Servant		No
Sarah Shingell	20	Female Servant		No
Anne Davies	15	Female Servant		No
Anne Pritchard	45	Female Servant		No

It is interesting to note that none of the male or the female servants were local or at least not born in this county. Often the Head of the household would purposely not employ servants who would live in and who could not go home at night and tittle tattle about the goings on at the 'big house'.

The next entry on this Census for Dumbleton village was for the *Rectory House* in the village where the *Rev. Samuel Gerrard* the Curate of the parish lived with his wife and six children. He ran a boarding school and 20 pupils were resident in the house on the night of the census.

The Old Rectory in the village of Dumbleton:-JRH©

The next census which includes Dumbleton Hall is dated 1851, the year of the *Great Exhibition* in London; Edward is shown as a widower at 45 years of age-*Landed Proprietor Born Austria with British parents*. At this time he has 7 children, the last being only 1 year of age, so he must have lost Sophia his wife only a short time before.

Census for Dumbleton 1851

Edward Holland	Head-Widower	Age 45	Landed Proprietor	Born: Austria
Sofia Holland	Daughter	16-unmarried		Dumbleton, Gloucestershire
Anne Caroline Holland	Daughter	11 - unmarried		Dumbleton, Gloucestershire
Mary Emily Holland	Daughter	9 - unmarried		Dumbleton, Gloucestershire
Swinton Colthurst Holland	Son	7		Dumbleton, Gloucestershire
Fanny Margaret Holland	Daughter	5		Dumbleton, Gloucestershire
Lucy Georgina Holland	Daughter	2		Dumbleton, Gloucestershire

43

Jessie Clara Holland	Daughter	1		Dumbleton, Gloucestershire
Harriet Isaac	Mother- in- Law - Widow	65		Quatt, Shropshire
Elizabeth Anne Isaac	Niece	5		Australia
Josephine Cobb Gilbertson	Governess	40 - unmarried		St Giles in the Field, Middlesex
Mary Cobb	Housekeeper	46 - unmarried		Stoorly, Devon
James Croft	Butler	44 - married		Lugwardine, Hereford
Mary Fenn	Nurse	42 - married		St James, Middlesex
Ellen Parkinson	House Maid	29 - unmarried		Boulton, Yorkshire
Ellen Griffiths	House Maid	21 - unmarried		Twyning, Gloucestershire
Ellen Stanley	Nurse	25 - unmarried		Overbury, Gloucestershire
Sarah James	Kitchen Maid	22 - unmarried		Dumbleton, Gloucestershire
Esther Spiers	Kitchen Maid	20 - unmarried		Ashton-under-Hill
Esther Hall	Nurse	19 - unmarried		Dumbleton, Gloucestershire
James Tilley	Footman	20 - unmarried		Esher, Surrey

In this census there do not appear to be any of the servants who have stayed on from 1841 and the number of indoor servants appears to be the same. Presumably they have moved on or retired. Others may not be registered who may have worked during the day part-time or when extra staffs were needed. Two examples would have been the laundry staff or when additional guests or family were staying at the hall. The children are all very young; it must have been a lively house to live in. The Mother- in- Law and the Holland niece are also living at the Hall at this time.

It is interesting to compare the number of servants working at the Hall at this time compared with the number of staff employed in the present 21ˢᵗ Century Hotel. A typical breakdown of today's staff would be:

32 full-time employees for the company
12 part -time staff – these include:

5 housekeeping
3 administration
1 maintenance

1 gardener
5 reception
7 kitchen,
17 restaurant/bar
5 management

Total 44

* *

It will be of interest here to look at what servants were employed at Dumbleton in Edward Holland's time and later into the Edwardian age. There was a strict hierarchy of the typical Victorian and Edwardian household:

The Valet:

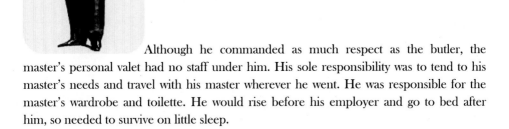

Although he commanded as much respect as the butler, the master's personal valet had no staff under him. His sole responsibility was to tend to his master's needs and travel with his master wherever he went. He was responsible for the master's wardrobe and toilette. He would rise before his employer and go to bed after him, so needed to survive on little sleep.

Each day he would need to check that his master had the correct outfit for each occasion, that it was pressed and ready to be worn and that his master's shoes and boots were always clean and polished, often with newly ironed shoelaces. In the morning he would shave his employer and make sure a bath was drawn and hot when required.

A valet had a special standing in the household of the important families, and would often be treated as a close friend and confidant of the head of the household. On shooting days on the larger estates he would have the responsibility of looking after the guns and loading his master's weapons, unless there was a 'loader' or 'under-keeper' to take on that role. On outings he would take charge of timetables and travel arrangements, as well as supervising the packing of the many cases and trunks needed when the family and his master travelled. If abroad he would be expected to know the local customs and even act as a translator if required. The valet was often very well connected and discreet, rather like the head porters of the top London hotels today.

The Butler:

During the Victorian period and later when household staff were not so easy to get, the Butler's position would become more important, especially if the role of Valet or house steward was no longer required or afforded.

The butler oversaw the running of the household and was directly in charge of the serving staff, footmen and hall staff and, therefore, also for their behaviour. He would be needed to liaise with the housekeeper on the duties of the kitchen staff and the household staff. He would be in charge of the wine cellar, the family silver in the house safe and oversee the smooth running of all the meals, keeping an eye on the footmen waiting at the tables to make sure they knew and used the correct etiquette at all times.

When the guests were being entertained he would have the responsibility of overseeing the menu and to choose the correct wine for each course, filling the glasses himself.

At lunchtime he might serve the meal alone, especially if only the family were present and at dinner he would be obliged to check that the starter was on the table ready before calling the family. It was his role to make sure the table was set exactly right and always looked good for the visiting guests but always perfect for the family themselves.

The Housekeeper:

The housekeeper's role at a large country house like Dumbleton, would be the head of the domestic staff, and she would run the establishment with military precision, every member of staff knowing their role and how to behave and the housekeeper would ensure this was always the case. She was in charge of the kitchen staff and the maids and was assisted in her domination by the cook and in some cases by the head housemaid. According to the 1825 householders' bible 'The Complete Servant', she should be a *'steady middle-aged woman, of great experience in her profession and a tolerable knowledge of the world.'*

One of her most important duties was to greet the master and mistress and the rest of the family when they returned home from a journey, or even a day out, by standing at the top of the staircase or inside the front door. She would also greet guests and show them to their rooms. She was in charge of the storerooms such as the china cupboards and linen cupboards and would keep keys for other rooms in the house. She was also the sole keeper of the 'still room' where the preserves, fruit wines and cordials were kept.

The housekeeper was always addressed as 'Mrs' whether she was married or not and often inspired more fear from the 'unders' than the mistress or the butler himself.

Lady's Maid:

The lady's maid was a luxury only the wealthier families could afford. She would like the Valet become a trusted and valued companion. Her duties were between a dresser and a sort of secretary and she needed to know about clothes and fashion as well as how to dress hair. Lady's maids had become a status symbol, especially if they knew about the latest French fashion and could advise their mistress.

The lady's maid would look after her employer's wardrobe, helping to choose and arrange clothes for particular occasions or events. With some society ladies, this could mean changing up to five times a day for various engagements, especially when the household would be in London during the 'season'. She had to be on hand to suggest lotions and beauty care. She would have the ear and the trust of the mistress and would naturally be discreet about anything she witnessed or overheard.

The Governess

In Victorian times, the children would be brought up by the Nanny of the household and the Governess who was responsible for their early education. Later the boys would attend a school such as Eton, Harrow, Westminster or a similar public school. By the turn of the century the girls would also be getting a more formal education.

The Governess had a strange position in the household as she was not considered to be in the same class as the family and also not a servant; her life could be a lonely one. She would be well educated and often as the unmarried daughter of a middle class or well to do family, who for some reason or other needed to gain employment-. We remember Charlotte Bronte's *Jane Eyre*. Elizabeth Gaskell, Henry's cousin and visitor to Dumbleton knew Charlotte and the Bronte family well.

Housemaids:

In the best houses both chambermaids and parlourmaids would be employed, as well as 'between-stairs maids' or 'tweenies' who performed duties in both the kitchen and the rest of the house, and the lowly maid-of-all-work. Parlourmaids were responsible for the reception rooms of the house, such as the drawing room, dining room, morning room and library, should there be one. She would dust and clean these rooms and lay the fire for each room. She would also wash woodwork, clean the lamps and polish the furniture in the room. The chambermaids had similar duties in the bedrooms, beginning each day by taking buckets of hot water and breakfast trays to the family and guests, then lighting the fires, making the beds, cleaning and dusting when the room was vacated.

The Cook:

There were two types of cook to be found in some of the wealthier houses, the professed cooks and plain cooks. The professed cook was an expert in creating the best menus for the family and for special parties and events. She would have under her a kitchen maid or under cook. She was not only responsible for cooking for the family and their guests but also for the servants' hall.

The cook was the absolute boss in the territory of the kitchen and many were just as feared and tyrannical as the housekeeper or the butler himself. She would meet at certain times with the mistress of the house to plan the daily menus or those special menus for parties and celebrations when the house could be full of guests and their own servants. Between mealtimes she would be preparing the food and helping in the making of jams, preserves, pastries and soups in advance and deal with the fruit and vegetables from the kitchen gardens and the game and meat from both the farms and shooting parties. She was always extremely busy and very highly regarded by the family. If the family had a London house or house abroad she would be one of the important servants who would travel with the family.

The Kitchen and the Scullery Maid:

The kitchen maid was the cook's closest assistant, and was employed to prepare all the ingredients before she started preparing the meal. She would chop vegetables, herbs and any meat that needed to be cut. She would also help with the cooking. She would cater for the other servants when the cook was busy preparing food for the family upstairs. She would also do the washing- up in the back kitchen.

The scullery maid also helped with the washing- up and cleaning the kitchen. She would light the kitchen fires in the morning and sweep the floors, clean the range and the flues and heat the hot water for cooking.

Footmen:

In the age of the carriage, footmen were an essential part of any rich household and some houses employed several. Dressed in high livery uniform, they would accompany the mistress or any of the family on the afternoon outings. In the evenings they would wait on table under the watchful eye of the butler.

By the beginning of the Twentieth century, many families swopped the role of footman to that of chauffeur when the family replaced their horses with cars.

Many families kept on the footmen as a show of wealth. Besides waiting at table they would often perform more general tasks such as cleaning the silver, carrying coal and announcing visitors.

Often the footmen were given a generic name, such as Henry or George, which would be used for every footman employed in the household.

Pageboy or Hall Boy:

PAGE BOY

He was at the bottom of the pecking order and was, in fact, the servant to the servants. He would not be allowed to set foot in the main house during the course of his duties and would be at the beck and call of the butler and the footmen at all times. The position of a Hall Boy could be taken by a local lad who still lived with his parents, or even a boy who would stay in the servants' quarters at the big house if he came from some distance away.

* *

It is during this period of the 1850s that Dumbleton became associated closely with **Elizabeth Gaskell**, who was of course a cousin to Edward and became close to his daughter Sophia. When the Hollands had guests to stay and were in residence too, it must have been a very full and lively household!

From Elizabeth's letters written at the time, we can learn quite a lot about her connection with **Dumbleton**, where she would come to stay for extended periods and work on her writing. She was a very profuse writer, of novels and of letters, many of which were written to celebrities of the time both in the field of literature and painting but also to people whom she admired or who had read her books.

She wrote from Dumbleton in 1856 to **Patrick Bronte,** the father of Charlotte Bronte. Later she wrote a biography of him. We know that in the 1850s Elizabeth contributed to

Charles Dickens's periodical 'Household Words' in every year from 1850 to 1858 apart from 1857 when she was concentrating on her '*Life of Charlotte Bronte*'. She is known to have also contributed to other Dickens's periodicals, and it is possible that some could have been written during her stay at Dumbleton. The periodicals included 'All Year Round' in 1859, 1861 and 1863.

Charles Dickens as a young man and later in life

Charles Dickens's family and friends c1864 – Charles Dickens, Jr., Kate Dickens, Miss Hogarth, Mary Dickens, Wilkie Collins, & Georgina Hogarth. Charles Dickens like Edward Holland had a large family of 10 children.

In 1857, Dickens had hired professional actresses for the play 'The Frozen Deep' which he and his protégé **Wilkie Collins** had written. Dickens fell deeply in love with one of the actresses Ellen Ternan, and his passion for her was to last for the rest of his life. Dickens was at the time 45 and Ellen only 18 when he made the decision, which went strongly against the Victorian convention of the time, to separate from his wife Catherine in 1858. Divorce, at this time, was unthinkable for someone as notable as Charles. When Catherine left, never to see her husband again, she took with her only one of the children, leaving the others to be raised by her sister Georgina who chose to stay at Gadshill in Kent.

Ellen Ternan in 1858 & Wilkie Collins (1824-1889)

Gadshill Place in Kent

We know from her letters that at this time she also stayed with Lady Kay Shuttleworth at Briary Close, Windermere. Here she met **Charlotte Bronte, Wordsworth** and also **Ruskin,** whose wife had been at the same school as herself.

Catherine Hogarth Dickens by Samuel Lawrence (1838)

William Wordsworth 1770-1850 & and John Ruskin 1819-1900

She was a great admirer of **Florence Nightingale** and several letters exist which give an idea of their friendship and respect for each other, and Elizabeth's admiration for the work of Florence at the Middlesex Hospital and in the Crimea. In fact part of 'North and South' was written at the Nightingale's house Lea Hurst near Matlock in Derbyshire. Some of the letters written by Elizabeth could presumably have been written while she was staying at Dumbleton.

Florence Nightingale and the statue erected in 1914 in Pall Mall, London by Arthur George Walker (1861-1939)

Elizabeth at this time enjoyed travelling and visiting her many friends including her stays with her cousin at **Dumbleton**. She spent family holidays at Silverdale on the coast of Morecambe Bay, but also visited Normandy in 1853, Rome in 1857 and 1863 and Germany in 1858 and 1860. It is interesting to note that in the 1861 Census, Edward and his second wife Frances Maria had a 29 year old German governess for their children at Dumbleton.

In 1857 Elizabeth was corresponding with the **Duke of Devonshire**, and after visiting Chatsworth House, was unexpectedly asked to stay. She had been writing to the Duke concerning her letters from **Charlotte Bronte.**

Chatsworth House, Derbyshire

Here we have mention of **Edward Thurston Holland** (1836-84), Edward's eldest son who had been on an extended visit to America and was engaged to be married to Elizabeth's daughter Marianne in 1866. Mrs Gaskell wrote glowingly of him '*He is so good and intelligent that I am sure (an American friend of hers) will like him at once...*' and was eager to see him after his visit to America in 1859. Thurston remained faithful to Marianne during a difficult courtship, opposed firstly because they were cousins and secondly because Marianne was 18 months older than he was. He was thought to be the son of a rich man but had eleven brothers and sisters, and had to make his own way in that most tedious of all professions 'Chancery Law' – source: 'Letters to Mrs Gaskell.

The marriage did take place just after Mrs Gaskell's death in 1866 and though the obligations to Dumbleton ended with the sale of the estate, he still kept in touch with the village sending cheques to poor widows and also coming up from London for the funeral of the village Rector his father had appointed, his second cousin Robert Wedgwood. **by** this time the Rector had left the Old Rectory and built himself a fine new house to the north of the village.

The Reverend Robert Wedgwood's fine marble tombstone in the village churchyard:-
JRH©

Elizabeth Gaskell also visited Ashbourne Gask in Derbyshire the home of Edward's other son **Frederick**. (Hewas born at Dumbleton and is shown on the 1841 Census as being one year old).

In 1859 Elizabeth visiting the **Duchess of Sutherland** and attended the Crystal Palace. Harriet, Duchess of Sutherland was the '*Mistress of the Robes*' for Queen Victoria and said to be one of the Queen's closest confidantes. It is at this time that she also mentions her visit to **Mr and Mrs Wordsworth** and his sister Dora, who were all living at Grasmere near Ambleside. Her comments are interesting, in that she speaks of the family being very poor. She mentions that while William would write in the mornings, his wife '*cooked and* *helped in the house'.* She would help to nurse and make up the beds – they had no servants and one small child at this time.

Mrs Gaskell also mentions her connection with **Dante Gabriel Rossetti** when she wrote in March of 1861. The following census for this period gives us an idea of the household at Dumbleton in this year when Mrs Gaskell would have visited.

Dante Gabriel Rossetti-1828-1882

By the time of the 1861 Census, Edward had married again. He is noted as being 55 years of age while his wife Frances Sophia is 36 so a 19 year difference in age.

Dumbleton 1861

Dumbleton Hall

	Age	Position	Married	Born
Edward Holland	55	Landed Proprietor	"	Austria/British
Frances Sophia Holland	36	Wife	"	Malta
Harriet Sofia Holland	26	Daughter	unmarried	Dumbleton
Edward Thurston Holland	25	Son-Law Student	unmarried	Dumbleton
Anne Caroline	21	Daughter	unmarried	Dumbleton

Holland				
Mary Emily Holland	19	Daughter	unmarried	Dumbleton, Gloucestershire
Swinton Colthurst Holland	17	Son – Midshipman in Royal Navy	unmarried	Dumbleton Gloucestershire
Frances Margaret Holland	13	Daughter		Dumbleton Gloucestershire
Lucy Georgina Holland	12	Daughter		Dumbleton Gloucestershire
Jessie Clara Holland	10	Daughter		Dumbleton Gloucestershire
Herbert Christian Holland	2	Son		London
Edith Jane Holland	1	Daughter		Dumbleton Gloucestershire
Henry Ewan Holland	6 months	Son		Dumbleton Gloucestershire
Louise Marie Wessel	29	Governess	unmarried	Germany
Jane Austin	38	Housekeeper	unmarried	Barthomley, Sussex
Elizabeth Eliza Reid	24	Lady's Maid	unmarried	London
Ann Heath	23	Lady's Maid	unmarried	Dumbleton Gloucestershire
Ann Pooke	32	House Maid	unmarried	Lumace Somerset
Letitia Grinnell	19	House Maid	unmarried	Dumbleton Gloucestershire
Eliza Brogan	18	Nursery Maid	unmarried	Belfast, Ireland
Hester Taylor	21	Kitchen Maid	unmarried	Frome Somerset
Anne Cooper	34	Wet Nurse	widow	Worcestershire
Eynes White	21	Footman	unmarried	Wychett Dorset

In this census it is interesting to note that Edward's son *Swinton Colthurst (1844-1922)* appeared on the 1851 census at Dumbleton aged 7 years, and ten years later in 1861 he is noted as being a Midshipman in the Royal Navy. He joined the Navy at just 13 years of age and had a very distinguished career, and was another of Edward's sons who was extremely successful in his chosen career. At the time of his death, '*The Times*' (10th June 1922) printed his obituary, which makes for some fascinating reading. This young boy who joined the Navy at only 13 years of age achieved so much:

Admiral Swinton Holland:-courtesy of Rob and Pam Mifflin©

DEATH OF ADMIRAL SWINTON HOLLAND

LETTERS TO 'THE TIMES' ON THE NAVY

'One of the most enlightened and talented naval officers of his generation has passed away in Admiral Swinton C. Holland, FRGS., whose death is announced on another page. The late Admiral often contributed to the columns of 'The Times' letters on such subjects as naval education and the training of seamen, which were invariably marked by sound judgement and breadth of outlook. While Admiral-Superintendent of Chatham Dockyard his interest in the past history of his profession, led him to found the Dockyard Museum there.

An Early View of Chatham Dockyard

Swinton Colthurst Holland was the third son of Mr Edward Holland, M.P., D.L., J.P., of Dumbleton Hall, Gloucester, and was born on February 8ᵗʰ 1844. He became a naval cadet in December 1844, and was made a sub lieutenant in September 1863 and a lieutenant two years later. His first ship after 'Malacca', in the Pacific, where he served between three and four years, and then had nearly as long a period in the surveying vessel 'Sylvia', in the China Seas. In February 1876, he was appointed flag-lieutenant to Vice-Admiral Sir A. Cooper Key, Commander- in- chief in North American waters, and when the Admiral hauled down his flag in the 'Bellerophon' in the spring of 1878, Holland was promoted to commander. In June, 1878, he was appointed commander of the 'Thunderer', on particular service, and in August 1880, of the 'Royal Adelaide,' flagship of the Commander-in-Chief at Devonport, which post he left the following April to become commander of the Royal yacht 'Victoria and Albert', the predecessor of the present vessel of the name.

Royal Yacht 'Victoria and Albert' - 1897

In accordance with custom, after three years in the yacht he was promoted captain on April 9ᵗʰ 1884. A period of study at the Royal Naval College, during which he was awarded the £50 prize for steam and naval architecture, followed, and he was then appointed flag-captain to Rear-Admiral (afterwards Admiral) the Hon. Sir E. R. Freemantle, Second- in – Command of the Channel Squadron, on December 1ˢᵗ, 1886. ......Captain continued as flag-captain under Rear-Admiral C. J. Rowley during 1887-88, and after a period on shore was appointed in command of the cruiser 'Australia' in the Mediterranean.

The Royal Naval College - Greenwich

On July 15th 1893, he took charge of the Fleet Reserve at Chatham – the same day, oddly enough, as that on which the late Lord Beresford was appointed Captain of the Steam Reserve at the same port. Here he spent three years, and in July 1896, received the appointment of Commodore-in-Charge at Hong-Kong. While in the Far East he was promoted to rear-admiral on January 1st 1899. Returning home, he became Admiral-Superintendent of Chatham Dockyard in September 1899, and occupied the post for three years. This proved to be his last appointment on the active list. He received advancement to vice-admiral in August 1903 and to admiral on June 1st 1907; on April 11th 1908, he was placed on the retired list (he was now 64 years of age – having spent over 50 years in the Royal Navy).

Admiral Holland married in 1881 (he was 37 years of age) to Miss Eva A. Williams, daughter of Commander Williams R.N., and had one son and two daughters. He was appointed a J.P. for Sussex in 1914.

The first part of his funeral service will be in Chichester Cathedral on Monday at 11 o' clock. He left a request that no flowers should be sent.'

Chichester Cathedral

'The Times' for the 14th June 1922 reported on his funeral:

FUNERAL – ADMIRAL SWINTON HOLLAND

'The ashes of the late Admiral Swinton Holland, whose body was cremated at Woking on Monday, were committed to the sea off the Nab lightship yesterday.

The ashes were taken from Portsmouth harbour to the point of burial in the destroyer 'Tarpon' and as she passed all warships lowered their flags to half-mast. The only private mourner present was Major Lindsell, Admiral Holland's son-in-law.......At the end of the service two naval buglers sounded the Last Post.' (Thanks to Mrs Sue Campbell for finding this article.)

* *

Elizabeth Gaskell's daughter Marianne, who was to marry Thurston, also wrote extensively and many of her letters have survived. In 1859 she mentions a stay at **Dumbleton:** '*Meta and I went back with Sophie and Eunice to Dumbleton where we spent 10 days.*'

84 Plymouth Grove, Manchester, the Gaskell home

On the 3rd March, she again writes from her family home at *Plymouth Grove* and mentions her happiness to be engaged to Thurston- and that their engagement had been kept secret for some weeks as they were short of money. Edward Holland had already put forward his objections in that although he was a rich man and Thurston his eldest son, he had 11 brothers and sisters and it was Edward's intention that all his property would be divided equally between them. The prospect of the marriage was therefore poor, but in the November of the same year, Mrs Gaskell died suddenly and 14 months later the couple were married. By the time of her death, with her works becoming immensely popular, Mrs Gaskell was a moderately well-to-do woman in her own right and she had made her daughters her literary heirs and executors. Thurston and Marianne could purchase a house in Wimbledon. Unfortunately Thurston died in 1884 at the early age of 48, so Marianne took their seven children to *Alfrick Court* in Worcester, and lived here until 1920.

Alfrick Court in Worcester (today converted into flats)

A brief description of the death of Thurston appeared in the *Leicester Chronicle & Mercury* on the 4th October 1884:

'*A franchise demonstration at Wimbledon on Saturday was marked by a sad and fatal incident'. Mr. E. Thurston Holland, the chairman of the Radical Society, who was to have presided, and met the procession on the common; but just before taking his place at the head, he fell to the ground and almost immediately expired.'*

Thurston was responsible for the Wimbledon Cottage Hospital which opened in 1870 with 8 beds. '*Edward Thurston Holland, was one of the founders and its first Honorary Secretary and Treasurer'. 'Thurston Road' in Wimbledon is named after him.*

It is interesting that just ten years before, Thurston's sister who had married Major Ryan of the 41st Regiment, Bengal Staff Corps, had died on November 24th 1874 at Lucknow in India.

Memorial plaque to Frances Margaret in Dumbleton Church:-JRH©

In the *Gloucester Journal* of 9th January 1875 appeared the following notice:

'*Great grief was caused to the deceased only a few weeks ago by the loss of a young married daughter, who died in India under distressing circumstances and whose babes have just been sent home to the house (Dumbleton Hall) in mourning.'*

Above **Frances Margaret's** plaque is the sad brass cross to Edward Holland's youngest son who died on a visit to Malta at the young age of only 11 years. He also died on Christmas Day 1871 which was another tragedy for the family.

Memorial cross to Henry Edward Holland 1860-1871:- JRH©

Another brief connection with **Dumbleton Hall** and Mrs Gaskell at this time was in 1861, when through her friendship with Canon Charles Richson, an energetic promoter of popular education, one of Thurston's younger brothers, **Frederick**, obtained an Anglican curacy in Ancoats, one of the worst slums in the Manchester area.

Ancoates in 1898

Eventually, Frederick became Vicar of *All Saints* and *St Lawrence*, Evesham and then Vicar of Overbury, a village a few miles from Dumbleton. He married first Penelope, daughter of Robert Martin of Overbury, and after her death in 1873, his second wife was Elinor, daughter of John Martin of Ledbury. Fred was killed in a climbing accident in Switzerland and there is a tablet to his memory in Overbury Church.

Lake of Thuner with the Niesen Mountain in the background

The moving plaque in memorial of Frederick is as follows:

'In Memory of the Rev. Frederick Whitmore Holland, M.A. Vicar of Evesham

2ⁿᵈ son of Edward HOLLAND Esquire M. P., of Dumbleton

He was born August 1ˢᵗ 1838 and married (1st) Penelope, younger daughter of Robert MARTIN Esquire of This Place and (2nd) Elinor TRAHERNE, eldest daughter of John MARTIN, Esquire, M.P. of Ledbury. He died very suddenly on the 26ᵗʰ August 1881 on the Niesen Mountain in Switzerland and is buried at Thun in that Country. 'Blessed are the pure in heart, for they shall see God'. Matt: V:8'

Overbury Church:-JRH©

Overbury Church, Frederick Holland's Memorial plaque and the grave of his first wife Penelope in the Churchyard:-JRH©

It is interesting to note that his son Edward Holland, named after his **Dumbleton** Grandfather, was also a keen agriculturalist and also attended Eton and Trinity College Cambridge. The memorial is in the Colwall Parish Church, Malvern.

Ledbury Guardian & Herefordshire Advertiser *Saturday 21st November 1916*
MEMORIAL SERVICE HELD IN PARISH CHURCH
SECOND LIEUTENANT EDWARD HOLLAND M.C.
A special
Ledbury Guardian
& Herefordshire Advertiser
Saturday 25th September 1916
SECOND LIEUTENANT EDWARD HOLLAND KILLED
Second Lieutenant Edward Holland, Scots Guards, formerly of Worcester Yeomanry, killed in action on September 15th was the younger son of the late Rev. Fred Whitmore Holland, vicar of Evesham. He was born in 1879 and educated at Eton and Trinity College, Oxford. on going down from Oxford he took up farming on the property at Old Colwall, Malvern which he inherited from his mother. He was owner and occupier of Old

Colwall Estate and the owner and occupier of Brick Farm and Moorcroft Farm. Since he acquired the estate he had taken an active interest in agriculture. He made a speciality of fruit farms and was reaping the benefit of judicious planting in the past.

Edward Holland was born in 1877 in Evesham where his father the Rev. Frederick Whitmore Holland was Vicar. His father died in 1881 and his mother Elinor Traherne Holland moved to Old Colwall. Her brother Waldyer Martin lived at The Upper Hall, Ledbury. When his mother died in 1903, Edward inherited Old Colwall. He served with the Worcester Yeomanry and was transferred to the Scots Guards. He was killed in action in Bernafay Wood during the Battle of the Somme in September 1916.
Edward Holland is commemorated on the Thiepval Memorial, at Eton College and at Coddington. Samuel Pugh and Albert James of Colwall are commemorated on the Thiepval Memorial as well.'

'**Ledbury Guardian & Herefordshire Advertiser** Saturday 21st November 1916

MEMORIAL SERVICE HELD IN PARISH CHURCH
SECOND LIEUTENANT EDWARD HOLLAND M.C.

A special service was held in memory of the Scots Guards on Friday at the hour fixed for the holding of a memorial service to the honour of the officers and men who had fallen in the Battle of the Somme in Holy Trinity Church, Sloane Square.
The deed which won the deceased Lieutenant the Military Cross was performed on September 13th last. After a raid in the night on the Guards' trenches while the Scots Guards were holding them, a patrol of 7 men and one officer was required to make a daylight reconnaissance and report on the enemy's position. Lieut. Holland volunteered for the task and the patrol accomplished its work. Whilst returning Lieut. Holland was hit in the back and died almost immediately. His men carried him in and buried him just outside the village. Previous to being transferred a few months ago to the Scots Guards Lieut. Holland served with the Queen's Own Worcestershire Hussars. The memorial service was attended by a large congregation. After the service muffled peels were rung at the church.'

It was Fred who officiates at his eldest sister's wedding at Dumbleton in 1865.

* *

In 1865 a great event took place at Dumbleton Hall. It was the wedding of Edward Holland's eldest daughter, Harriet Sophia Holland who was 26 at the time of the 1861 Census. She would have been in her early thirties when her marriage took place at Dumbleton. Her father, Edward, had been married twice and had 14 children- at least 8 girls with the bride and the 7 of the 14 bridesmaids for this fine family event.

The event was written up in the local newspaper and appears to be a very jolly and happy affair, which would have caused much excitement for the family and the village of Dumbleton.

'The Marriage of Miss Holland of Dumbleton

On Tuesday last, Dumbleton the seat of Edward Holland Esq. MP was the scene of a very interesting event, namely the wedding of Miss Harriet Sophia Holland, Mr Holland's eldest daughter, with Crompton Hutton Esq. of Putney Park, Middlesex.

The bride is much beloved and respected wherever she is known, those feelings culminating in her native village, where her virtues are best known, and where her efforts for the good of the villagers and the education of the poor, are spoken of in the warmest and most grateful tones.

The Church at Dumbleton is sited at the edge of the park, and is approached from the Hall by a graceful winding carriageway terminating at the entrance to the Churchyard in a path overhung with trees and evergreens. Along this pathway garlands and wreaths were suspended in profusion, while the chancel arch of the Church, the altar rails and altarpiece and other parts of the chancel were decorated with flowers of the rarest and most beautiful kind, and arranged with great taste.

A flag waved from the summit of the old tower. The village was decorated with flowers and flags and at the entrance to the Hall, an arch of evergreens was erected.

The bride and groom with the fourteen bridesmaids: - courtesy of Mr Martin Grafton-Archivist©

Shortly after eleven o' clock the happy bridegroom, Mr Crompton Hutton accompanied by his brother Mr Stanford Hutton as 'best man' preceded to the church, and they were speedily followed by the procession of bridesmaids, fourteen in number, who walked from the Hall to the Church, and who in their native beauty and elegant attire, formed as they came down the slope of the hill as pretty a sight as one could wish to see.

After the bridesmaids came a group of ladies and gentlemen, members and friends of the family. The bride accompanied by her father, was driven from the Hall in a carriage and pair of greys, and followed by her fair bevy of bridesmaids, preceded to the altar, where the bridegroom was already waiting. The marriage service was performed by the Rev. Frederick Whitmore Holland (brother of the bride) assisted by the Rev R. Wedgwood.

At the close of the ceremony, the bridal party proceeded back to the Hall, the bride's path being strewed with flowers, good omens it is hoped of the happiness of her future. At the Hall an elegant 'dejeuner' supplied by Mr George of Cheltenham, and reflecting the highest credit on his taste and skill, was served under the superintendence of Mr Brown and Mr Locke.

Groups of visitors in holiday attire dotted the park and gardens, the latter appearing to great advantage, speaking well for Mr Edwards's attention and skills. The merry bells pealed forth from the old tower, and the strains of the Evesham Rifle Corps Band added to the festivity of the occasion.'

The Old Church and Tower in Dumbleton Village:-JRH©

An early view of the Church at Dumbleton: - courtesy of the Dumbleton Society and the Late Don Caisey©

.....Tea was provided for the schoolchildren in the park, and in the course of the afternoon, the happy pair left for Ross, with the congratulations and best wishes for their happiness of the assembled company. The wedding presents were very numerous, costly and elegant.

* *

Edward Holland died in 1875 after owning Dumbleton Hall for over 45 years. The 'Berrow's Worcester Journal' for the 9th January 1875 printed the following obituary which gives an interesting insight into the life of Edward who had built Dumbleton and enjoyed living here with his family for many years of his busy life:

'THE LATE MR. EDWARD HOLLAND

It is our painful duty to record the death of Mr. Edward Holland, who expired on Monday last at his residence, Dumbleton Hall, near Evesham, at the age of sixty-nine. His decease has excited widespread regret, for he was known and respected far beyond the confines of the two counties with which he was more closely connected. He had long occupied a foremost place in the rank of British agriculturalists, and to so large extent did he possess their confidence and esteem, that he had enjoyed the highest honours which the Royal Agricultural Society could confer upon him. He had for some time lived in comparative retirement. Seven years ago he relinquished the active role he had for a long period taken in political matters as a member of the Legislature, but his interest in agricultural improvements remained unimpaired. The immediate cause of death was congestion of the lungs. Mr. Holland was apparently in his usual state of health up to Saturday last, when he caught cold, and on the Sunday evening the symptoms were of so severe a character that no hope of recovery was entertained. The deceased gentleman was a son of the late Mr. Swinton Colthurst Holland, of the great house of Barings. He was born in 1806, and educated at Eton and Trinity College, Cambridge, where he graduated as B.A. and M.A. in due course. He married, firstly, Sophia, second daughter of the late Mr. Elias Isaac, of Boughton House, who died in 1851 and in 1857 for his second wife Frances Maria, daughter of the late Mr. Samuel Christian of Malta. He leaves a large family. His eldest son, Mr Thurston Holland, is a Chancery barrister; his second son, Rev. F. W. Holland is the vicar of All Saints in Evesham. Mr. Edward Holland was a magistrate for the counties of Gloucestershire and Worcestershire and served the office of High Sheriff of the latter county in 1842. His political career extended over a period of nearly 45 years. In January 1835 he was elected in the Liberal interest as a member for East Worcestershire. In July 1855 he was elected without opposition for the borough of Evesham, for which he continued to sit until 1868, when the borough was deprived of one of its members and he had then decided to withdraw from Parliamentary life.

......It was as an agriculturalist, however that Mr. Holland was known to fame and that his memory will long be cherished with pride and affection. No nomination to the presidency of the Royal Agricultural Society ever received a heartier welcome than was accorded to that of Mr. Holland in 1873. He was an original member of the society, and had been a member of its council for many years.. He was an early advocate and promoter of steam cultivation, and had long been a successful breeder of Shropshire sheep, which indeed owed their position as a distinctly-acknowledged separate breed and class very much to his energetic advocacy of their merits. Agriculturalists owe to him one of the most careful definitions of the relationship between landlords and tenants that have ever been drawn up. But it was in connection with the subject of agricultural education that his most

valuable services were rendered. He was prominently associated with the foundation of the Royal Agricultural College at Cirencester. He was the president of the College, and only two or three weeks ago attended to distribute the prizes awarded to the pupils. That this institution survived the misfortunes of its early years was attributed to his self-denying exertions; and that the Royal Agricultural Society has continued, under considerable discouragement to make its annual contribution to the promotion of agricultural education in this country is due very much to his know n wishes and urgent efforts. It was universally conceded at the time of his nomination to the presidency of the Royal Society that no one could have been named having better claims to the distinction, and that the council never more perfectly anticipated the wishes of the members.

In agriculture, as in politics, Mr. Holland was a mass of advanced thought and practice, but so great was his personal popularity that, notwithstanding his advocacy – always open and fearless – of views which were often distasteful to farmers, no man was more respected among that class than he was. He was actively connected, both in his locality and in London, with the agitation for the abolition of the Corn Laws and he lived to remind the farmers, which he frequently did, of that he conceived to be the beneficent results of the policy he had promoted.........

In a view to the advancement of local agriculture, Mr. Holland devoted, for many years, a large amount of capital and skill to the maintenance of a model farm at **Dumbleton,** *where the most modern machinery and improvements of every description were adopted.* **Dumbleton** *was a pattern village, and the labourers, receiving fair wages and kind treatment are most contented with their lot; each man has a capital home, with a large garden and good water supply; and by the generous policy which he adopted, Mr. Holland solved many of the difficulties which beset the labour question. He was the mainstay of the* **Evesham Agricultural Society,** *which once held so important a place among the district associations owing to his wise counsels and zealous efforts. Of the county societies of Worcester and Gloucester he was an ardent supporter. In past times, when the Worcestershire Society held its annual shows under restrictions that have passed away, he was distinguished by an earnest support of improvements both in the breeding of stock and in the cultivation of the soil. In 1838 the society first instituted premiums for stock. In the following year Mr. Holland had prizes for sheep, and, as frequently the case at subsequent shows, won them with his own animals. When under the new constitution, the annual exhibition was held at Evesham, Mr Holland most efficiently fulfilled the duties of president in the absence of* **H.R.H. the Duc d' Aumale, (** *see book on 'Wood Norton' by John Hodges), who had been appointed to this office.*

The deceased gentleman will be greatly missed in Evesham and in the neighbourhood, for he took an active interest in local affairs, as chairman of petty sessions, president of the Evesham Institute from its commencement, of the Winchcombe Agricultural Society, and other institutions. The funeral took place at Dumbleton today (Friday).

'The Berrow's Worcester Journal' printed an article on the funeral of Edward Holland on Saturday January 16ᵗʰ 1875:

'THE LATE MR. EDWARD HOLLAND

The mortal remains of the above gentleman were interred in the family vault at Dumbleton on Friday. The cortege left **Dumbleton Hall** *shortly before one o'clock, the following being among those present:*

Mourners: Mr. Thurston Holland, Rev. F. W. Holland, Mr and Mrs Crompton- Hutton, Miss G. Holland, Master H. Holland, Mr and Mrs J. Whitmore Isaac, Mr Geo. Holland, Mrs. Croft, Col. J. Macinroy, Mrs Thurston Holland, Mr George Christian, Capt. Christian, Rev. Lister Isaac, Rev. Powis Isaac, Mr Roberts, Miss Isaac, Mrs and Misses Wedgwood.

Tenancy: Mr C. Randell (steward), Mr J. Smith, Mr W.A. Corbett, Mr B. Smithin, Mr. C. Morris, Mr Chas. Walker..............................

The coffin (without pall) was carried on a bier underhanded by eight servants of the family. The service of the dead was impressively read by the rector, the Rev. R. Wedgwood, and the body was committed to the earth amid manifestations of grief by all present, including many poor people, who were deeply affected on losing one of their best friends. The coffin was placed in the family vault, which already contained the remains of the deceased's mother, who died in the year 1845, his first wife Sophia, who died in 1851, his daughter, Susan Florence, who died in 1852, and his granddaughter, Agnes Sylvia (Mr. Thurston Holland's daughter).

The Holland Family Vault at Dumbleton Church: - JRH©

The coffin was made by Mr. Welch of **Dumbleton,** *consisting of a shell, enclosed in a lead coffin, and a polished oak outer coffin, brass furniture, and a plate, bearing the inscription:*

'Edward Holland'

Born 11th February 1806

Died Jan. 4th 1875'

On the coffin were beautiful wreathes and crosses of white camellias and other hothouse flowers, and after it was placed in the vault it was covered with bouquets by loving hands.

The Water Fountain erected close to the Church in memory of Edward Holland by his close friends, including the Wedgwood family whose famous pottery is known all over the world:-JRH©

On his demise his eldest son Thurston inherited the hall and the estate, but he decided to sell both for £180,000 (Present money). Thurston had little choice but to sell the Hall and Estate as his father's' will had divided his estate between his children. The Sales catalogue from this period makes for some interesting reading.

FIRST EDITION.

GLOUCESTERSHIRE,

ON THE BORDERS OF WORCESTERSHIRE.

Particulars and Conditions of Sale

OF THE

"DUMBLETON HALL ESTATE,"

ONE OF THE MOST COMPACT AND DESIRABLE

FREEHOLD RESIDENTIAL PROPERTIES IN ENGLAND,

Situate in the Parishes of Dumbleton, Beckford, and Ashton-under-Hill, One and a half Miles from Ashton-under-Hill and Two-and-a-half Miles from Beckford Stations, on the Midland Railway, equi-distant Five Miles from Evesham and Winchcombe, Eight-and-a-half from Tewkesbury, and only Ten from Cheltenham. It comprises a

SUBSTANTIAL STONE-BUILT MANSION,

Containing the necessary Accommodation for a Family of Distinction, seated on rising ground, surrounded by

CHARMING PLEASURE GROUNDS,

ORNAMENTAL PLANTATIONS,

AND A

WELL - TIMBERED PARK.

IN ADDITION ARE

SEVERAL FIRST-CLASS FARMS,

WITH

SUPERIOR RESIDENCES AND GOOD HOMESTEADS,

Corn Mill, Brickyard, numerous Small Occupations, and Cottages,

INCLUDING (WITH A SMALL EXCEPTION)

THE WHOLE OF THE VILLAGE OF DUMBLETON

AND THE

WELL-ARRANGED SCHOOLS, WITH TEACHER'S RESIDENCE,

EMBRACING ALTOGETHER AN AREA OF

2,182 a.   O r.   35 p.,

INTERSPERSED WITH

EXTENSIVE AND WELL-GROWN

WOODS AND PLANTATIONS;

Also the Manors or Reputed Manors of Dumbleton and Didcot, with their Rights and Privileges, and

The Advowson or Right of Perpetual Presentation to the Rectory of Dumbleton.

The whole of which will be Offered for Sale by Auction by

Direction of the Trustees under the Will of the late Edward Holland, Esq., by

MESSRS. BEADEL,

AT THE MART, TOKENHOUSE YARD, LONDON, E.C.,

ON THURSDAY, THE 22nd DAY OF JULY, 1875,

AT ONE O'CLOCK PRECISELY, IN ONE LOT.

Particulars and Conditions of Sale may be obtained of Messrs. MAYNARD & SON, 57, Coleman Street, London; CHARLES RANDELL, Esq., Land Agent, Chadbury, near Evesham; and of Messrs. BEADEL, 25, Gresham Street, London, E.C., who will issue Orders to View, on application.

PARTICULARS.

The Dumbleton Hall Estate forms part of the fertile and far-famed Vale of Evesham. From the Mansion and Park are beautiful Views, extending over richly timbered valleys, and beyond, embracing Bredon Hill, the Malvern and Cotswold Hills, and other well-known Ranges.

The Society in the neighbourhood is everything which can be desired, Dumbleton Hall being in immediate contiguity to several first class Residential Estates.

The opportunities for Sporting are exceptionally good, the Estate is well stocked with winged game, and the covers afford every facility for preserving.

Earl Coventry's and the North Cotswold Foxhounds hunt the District.

THE MANSION

KNOWN AS

"DUMBLETON HALL"

IS A

SUBSTANTIAL STONE-BUILT STRUCTURE,

OF TUDOR DESIGN,

Seated on Rising Ground in the midst of a

WELL-TIMBERED PARK,

Partially encircled with

ORNAMENTAL PLANTATIONS.

THE INTERIOR ACCOMMODATION IS AS FOLLOWS:

ON THE GROUND FLOOR.

Entrance Hall, 37ft. 6in. by 24ft. 6in ; Small Drawing Room, 24ft. 6in. by 22ft. 6in. ; Drawing Room, 34ft. 6in. by 27ft., (including Bay) ; Conservatory, 60ft. by 20ft. ; Library, 29ft. 3in. (including Bay), by 25ft. ; Dining Room, 34ft. 6in. by 27ft. 6in. ; School Room, 23ft. 9in. by 17ft. 6in. ; W. C.

All these Apartments have an elevation of 16 feet. The principal Reception Rooms are decorated with exquisite taste, and, communicating with each other, form a continuous Suite. The Drawing Room opens into the Conservatory.

A Handsome Oak Staircase, with Gallery, and lighted from the Roof, conducts from the Entrance Hall to the

FIRST FLOOR.

The Ladies' Room, 29ft. 6in. (including Bay), by 24ft. 6in. ; South Turret Bed Room, 27ft. 6in. (including Bay) by 24ft. ; ditto Dressing Room, 17ft. by 10ft. ; Oak Bed Room, 22ft. 6in. by 17ft. ; ditto Dressing Room, 17ft. by 7ft. ; Green Bed Room, 18ft. by 12ft. ; Ditto Dressing Room, 18ft. by 10ft. ; North Turret Bed Room, 27ft. 3in. (including Bay) by 24ft., with Staircase, Leading to No. 8 ; ditto Dressing Room, 17ft. by 10ft. 3in. ; East Bed Room, 23ft. by 17ft.

All these Rooms are 12ft. high.

SECOND FLOOR.

Bed Room No. 1, 23ft. by 7ft. 3in. ; No. 2, 24ft. by 12ft. 6in. ; No. 3, 22ft. 3in. by 14ft. 3in. ; No. 4, 17ft. 3in. by 10ft. ; No. 5, 20ft. by 18ft. ; No. 6, 23ft. by 14ft. ; No. 7 (Day Nursery), 24ft. 6in. by 24ft. 6in : No. 8 (Night Nursery), 21ft. 6in. by 14ft. 3in., communicating with No. 9, 20ft. by 17ft. 9in.

All these Rooms are 8ft. 10in. high.

IN WING.

Bath Rooms, fitted with hot and cold supply, three Bed Rooms, Store Room, Housemaid's Closet, and two W. C's.

THE DOMESTIC OFFICES

Include Butler's Pantry, with Bed Room and Plate Closet, Housekeeper's Room, dry Store Room, Office, Servants' Hall, Lamp Room, Kitchen, Scullery, three Larders, and excellent Cellarage.

The House is effectively heated on every floor with hot air.

THE OUT-OFFICES

Comprise Brew, Bake, and Boot Houses, Lumber Room, Fresh Meat Larders, three-stall Stable, Aviaries, &c., &c.

2

Sales details from the Dumbleton Estate in 1875:-courtesy of the Gloucester Archives©

There was a Codicil to the Will of Edward Holland which makes for some interesting reading:

'Codicil dated 24ᵗʰ October 1870

'He settled the sum of £5000 on the marriage of his son Frederick Whitmore Holland with Miss Penelope Martin and he likewise settled the sum of £2000 upon the marriage of his daughter Frances Margaret with Captain William C. B. Ryan now he declares that such sums shall be considered as parts of or as a whole as the case may be of the respective shares of his said son and daughter in his residuary estate. If after his death it is found that his daughter Frances Margaret shall be entitled to any further sum.

Whereas some years ago the late Captain Francis Holland gave his daughter Mary Emily Holland, to whom she was god-daughter, the sum of £750. This sum was paid to Edward Holland but by oversight it was invested in the name of his daughter Anna Caroline. This is to be regarded as part of the share of his daughter Anna Caroline in his residual estate and his executors are to pay Mary Emily £750 with interest at the rate of 4% from 6ᵗʰ August 1845 to be considered in the nature of a debt.'

* *

Chapter Four: Dumbleton Hall - the House & Gardens

In this Chapter I have looked at the House and the gardens which were originally laid out in the time of Henry Holland after 1830 and extended and altered in the early part of the 20th Century by Viscount Eyres-Monsell and his wife Lady Monsell. I have explained the progression of the house and gardens as shown on the early Ordnance Survey maps illustrated in this chapter from 1833 in the time of Henry Holland to the changes shown in 1923 at the time of the Eyres-Monsells.

In 1830 Edward Holland commissioned the building of the new Dumbleton Hall; he had bought the estate for an estimated £18,000. (In 1830, £18,000 0s 0d would have the same spending worth of 2005's £890,820.00-National Archives Converter.)

Edward employed *George Stanley Repton* to design his new home and the attached pleasure gardens.

Humphrey Repton and John Nash

George Stanley Repton, architect, was born on the 30th January 1786 and was the youngest son of *Humphrey Repton* (1752-1818). Early in his career Repton became a pupil of the London architect *John Nash* and his first work was the *Royal Opera House, Haymarket*, in London which he undertook as a pupil of Nash.

The Royal Opera House- Haymarket- London

After 1820 Repton practised independently as an architect and over the next twenty-five years worked on twenty-five commissions. These were largely made up of country houses in the *Greek, Palladian and Gothic revival styles*. Alterations to existing buildings made up two-thirds of his work and only ten were wholly built to his designs. Commissions included *Kitley House* which was remodelled in the Elizabethan style and *Peamore House*, Exeter, which was in the Tudor Gothic (Both houses were in Devon).

Kitley House & Peamore Hotel are in Devon. Like Dumbleton, today all are fine hotels

84

Peamore House in Devon

He lived his last thirteen years of his life in retirement and he died at his home on the 29th June 1858 at 27 New Norfolk Street, Park Lane, London.

Part of Norfolk Street, off Park Lane in London c1925

George Stanley Repton was, besides Dumbleton, associated with working on the following projects:

• Blaise Castle

• Blaise Hamlet

- Camerton Court

- Cobham Hall

- Hollycombe House

- Moccas Court

- Nanteos

- Rheola

- Sarsden House

- Witley Court

- Wolterton Hall

History of the Gardens for Dumbleton Hall

The garden would have been laid out after the creation of the Hall in the 1830s. From the different Ordnance Survey maps one can see the layout of the gardens and the changes which have taken place through time.

The garden which can be seen on the OS maps was enlarged between the Ordnance Survey visits of 1883 and 1923. The lake below the Hall did not exist in 1883. However, the pools feeding the lake had been built. The boathouse also existed in 1923.

OD Map of 1833 and 1923

The fountain, that still survives, appearing on the 1923 map, was a pool in 1883.

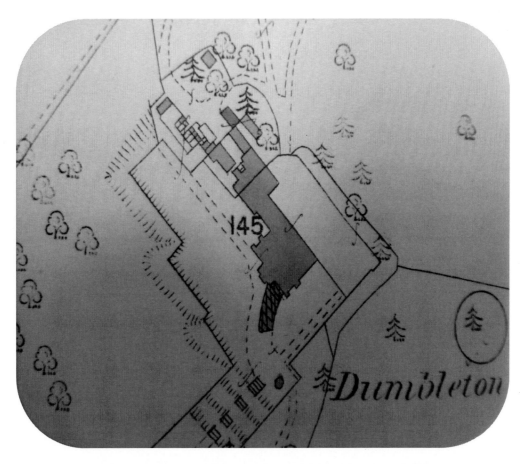

The 1883 OS Map of Dumbleton: courtesy of OS and Sue Campbell©

The filled in pool and the remains of the fountain in 2015

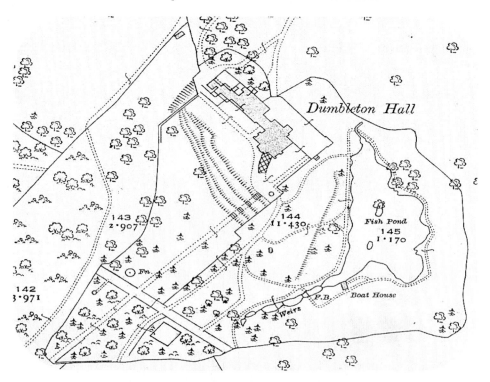

OS Map of Dumbleton 1923:-courtesy of OS and Sue Campbell©

The entrance to the rather overgrown boathouse in October 2014:-JRH©

Close to the southern boundary of the garden directly south of the Hall a hedged sheltered area had been grown by 1923. It was square shaped. An oblong shaped hedged area had been added to the south-east of this to surround a pool by 1981.

The kitchen gardens, which still existed in 1923, were at SP 0164 3600 though they were built over by 1998.

Detail from an early sketch of Dumbleton Hall: - courtesy of the 'Dumbleton Society & the late Don Caisey©

The Kitchen Garden at Dumbleton:-courtesy of The Dumbleton Society and the late Don Caisey©

The Kitchen Gardens were sited to the north-west of the village. They included hothouses and cold frames, enormous water tanks, and a typical 19th Century kitchen garden whose vegetables, fruit and flowers supplied the great house and also the village itself. The Head Gardener's house can be seen in the photograph:- courtesy of The Dumbleton Society & the late Don Caisey©

The kitchen garden and four of the gardeners outside one of the greenhouses at Dumbleton Hall: - courtesy of the Dumbleton Society & the late Don Caisey©

The lake was dug out and the boathouse was incorporated between 1887 and 1923 and from 1902 to 1905 there was a major rebuilding project, when the North wing was added to give extra staff and guest rooms. The architect was probably *Sidney Kitson of Bedford & Kitson of Leeds*. The east lodge and its adjacent cast iron gates were by *A. N. Prentice*.

The impressive cast iron gates to Dumbleton Hall in October 2014:-JRH

Sidney Decimus Kitson (1871-1937) – was born in 1871 and educated at Charterhouse and Trinity College, Cambridge. He was articled to Edward John May from 1893 to 1896, and he was the assistant to William Douglas Caroe in 1896. He commenced independent practice in 1896 in Leeds. Kitson worked in partnership with Francis William Bedford from 1897 to 1904. He was elected FRIBA on 3rd December 1906, his proposers being Edward John May, John Belcher and Harry Sutton Chorley. Prior to the First World War he had an extensive local practice.

Early view of the South Lodge:-courtesy of the Dumbleton Society and the late Don Caisey©

91

Andrew Noble Prentice (1866-1941)

From November 1883 to 1888 Andrew remained as assistant for a few months after completing his apprenticeship. In the latter year he won the *Soane Medallion,* which together with family money enabled him to undertake extensive travels in the following two years. He set off in February 1889, his first port of call being Malta, after which he toured Italy, Sicily and France. He returned in August 1889 and it appears that he may have made an enquiry about entering the RA Schools at that time: he was certainly in contact with R. Phené Spiers, who advised him to undertake a further study tour, this time of Spain, which lasted from November of that year until June 1890. R. Phene Spiers was responsible for the building of *Impney Hall* (later renamed *Chateau Impney*) for *John Corbett - The Worcestershire Salt King.* (See John Hodges's book – 'Chateau Impney - the Story of a Victorian Country House.)

Chateau Impney, near Droitwich, the home of John Corbett – The Worcestershire Salt King: courtesy of John Hodges©

His studies in Spain were published in 1893 as the folio '*Renaissance Architecture and Ornament in Spain*', dedicated to the *Queen Regent, Dona Maria Christina.* On his return from Spain he obtained a place in the office of Thomas Edward Collcutt and he passed the qualifying exam in March 1891, enabling him to be admitted to the ARIBA on 8 June of that year, his proposers being *Collcutt, Spiers and Leiper.*

Prentice was elected FRIBA on 3 February 1902, again with the support of Collcutt and Spiers but this time with Aston Webb as his third proposer. From 1920 until 1933 he was in partnership with William M. Dean and from 1935 until 1940 with H. J. Scaping and Arthur Henry Wheatley.

Prentice built many Arts and Crafts houses in Gloucestershire and Worcestershire. His work was characterized by exceptional refinement. His brother Thomas was a shipowner and much of his practice consisted of steamship interiors for the Orient and the Australian and South American Lines.

Prentice died at Willow Park in his native Greenock on 23 December 1941.

The South Lodge and the fine gates to the Hall, August 2014:-JRH©

The North Lodge with its avenue of trees leading to the Hall was the original entrance to Dumbleton Hall. Today the lodge has been extended to make a very fine 21st Century family home: - courtesy of Mr and Mrs Clark©

The original driveway to Dumbleton Hall. The few trees are all that is left today of the avenue planted in Edward Holland's time:-JRH©

The North Lodge in January 2015:-courtesy of Mr and Mrs Clark©

Dumbleton Hall in August 2014 showing the lighter extension of the north wing, added from c1902-1905:-JRH©

In 1959 after being placed on the market by Lady Eyres-Monsell, Dumbleton was sold to The Post Office Fellowship of Remembrance for use as a convalescent and holiday home.

An early photograph showing the lake with the boathouse at the far end and the gravelled path alongside the lake: courtesy of Mr Martin Grafton-archivist©

The gravelled paths leading to the lake and the large splendid conservatory can be clearly seen: - courtesy of Mr Martin Grafton – archivist©

Almost the same view of the Hall, but in 2014 the gravelled paths and fine flower beds have all gone and are now laid to grass for easy maintenance:-JRH©

Early photograph of Dumbleton c1914/20 showing the ornate ornamental flower beds and the fine planting in the stone pots with the gardeners hard at work. Note the conservatory with the tiled roof:- courtesy of Mr Martin Grafton-Archivist©

Note this earlier view of the Conservatory with the original glass roof: - courtesy of Mr Martin Grafton- Archivist©

The terrace steps at Dumbleton:-JRH©

The Hall and Gardens c1905:-courtesy of the Dumbleton Society & the late Don Caisey© (see colour plate)

The Staff at Dumbleton Hall c1907:- courtesy of the Dumbleton Society and the late Don Caisey©

In the spring the grounds of Dumbleton come alive with spring bulbs (see the colour plates for a view today of the spring flowers)

Photographs of Dumbleton Hall with the massed herbaceous beds laid out in the 20s and 30s:- courtesy of the Dumbleton Society and the late Don Caisey©

The main entrance to the Hall c1940:- courtesy of the Dumbleton Society and the late Don Caisey©

What was life like for the staff at Dumbleton Hall in Edwardian Times and the Early Twentieth Century?

Life at Dumbleton in the time of Edward Holland was very different to the Dumbleton of today, but being a hotel there are still many people involved in looking after the house and the guests who come to stay here.

Radio Gloucester gave interviews in the 1990s and these have been recorded and lent to me by Martin Grafton the archivist of Dumbleton Hall. They make for some interesting listening and I have transcribed some of these talks. It gives a picture of life in a great country house of the period and how the main house and the village worked together to support and help each other as a large extended family, which even today is still the case as many local people still work on the Dumbleton Estate in various capacities.

In the radio broadcast the Butler, Thomas Spencer, who was 96 years of age and his wife, who was the head cook at the Hall during the 1930s give an insight into the village and the Hall at this time.

He speaks of the Hall, village and family like a small Welfare State; the Dumbleton Estate provided employment and looked after their people. Milk from the dairy, eggs from the hens and whatever they needed were supplied to them.

Thomas spoke of life in the Hall which he had enjoyed a great deal and had always spoken highly of the kind family he worked for at the time. When he was Butler, he was in overall charge of 15 resident servants which included two footmen, a housekeeper, cooks and four kitchen maids. His role was to keep the rest of the staff in order, to arrange and work with the housekeeper and cook in organising the meals and accommodation for the family and their guests. He was in charge of the wine cellar and looking after the silver. There was a massive safe in the cellar where this was securely locked away, and the hall had extensive cellarage for the wine and for other foods including the game. The cellars were especially full after one of Lord Monsell's famous shooting parties.

Part of the extensive cellarage under Dumbleton Hall: - JRH©

The wine cellar in 2014:-JRH©

A photograph of the staff of a typical country house such as Dumbleton which included the Butler, Housekeeper, the lady's maid and Housemaids, the Cook and Scullery maids, Footmen and Hall boys. (the bottom of the pecking order and on call to all the other indoor staff).

Victorian Servants-graphic taken from '*The True Story of Life Below Stairs.*'

104

The outdoor staff would have included the servants such as grooms who looked after the horses and carriages as in Edward Holland's time and the motor mechanic and chauffeur of the Eyres-Monsell period.

The stable staff including the stable lads, grooms and carriage livery men as would have been at Dumbleton during the time of the Hollands:-courtesy of 'The Dumbleton Society' & the late Don Caisey©

The badge on the front of the massive iron safe and entrance to the cellar where barrels and other provisions for the Hall could be brought down to the cellars;-JRH©

Thomas mentions that during the war, he joined the police, but found that life outside Dumbleton was not so polite and kind. He states that he always found working for the Eyres-Monsell family a great honour.

The broadcast mentions the Head cowman, who was responsible for Lady Monsell's prize herd of Jersey cows. His name was Fred Nerdon and he was the father of six children. He married the cook Elsie from the Hall and she gives an insight into life for her and the other servants in the Hall.

Elsie remembered that there was always a lot of work to be done. The old coal fired range was where she cooked the family meals and meals for the many shooting and other parties which the Hall put on. Many famous guests came to stay over the years. She used to up and start work by 6.30 a.m with breakfast at 8.00a.m.

Elsie mentions that the family always enjoyed fine food, which of course the servants also shared. They all ate lots of game and they lived really well. She mentions travelling down to Lord Monsell's London home, in the back of his Lagonda with the valet and chauffeur-she noticed how terribly handsome Lord Monsell was and how much she respected and liked him. She remembers Lord Monsell's Rolls-Royce and a wonderful little two seater car which he would drive at speed up and down the drive with the ladies, making them squeal with pleasure. They would call at the dairy for some fresh cream before returning to the hall for lunch.

1930s style Lagonda

The Conservatory in August 2014:-JRH

An early photograph of the Conservatory c1910/20: courtesy of Mr Martin Grafton –Archivist©

Early postcard of Dumbleton Hall and the Hall today:-courtesy of the 'Dumbleton Society' and the late Don Caisey©

The herbaceous beds would have been created after 1830 as was the fine stone balustrade and other features which can be seen today.

The Palisade looking towards the lake and the fine Cedar of Lebanon-Feature created:
1830 to 1840:-JRH©

The ornamental Lake with its boathouse and islands. Here also breed black swans
originally donated by a member of the Post Office Fellowship Remembrance Society:-
JRH©

The beautiful garden enclosed with a fine yew hedge. One can see the outline of the swimming pool which was here in the 1930s.

Another charming 'secret' garden with a feature group at the centre. The walling was restored by Post Office Fellowship of Remembrance Chairman Mr Alan Bealby and his wife Sheena - JRH©

In 1862 the East window of Dumbleton Church was replaced. The masonry from the earlier window was set up at the Hall as a romantic ruin beside the lake:-JRH©

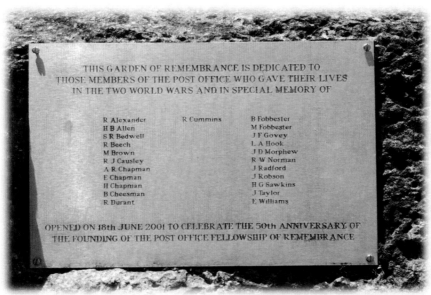

THIS GARDEN OF REMEMBRANCE IS DEDICATED TO
THOSE MEMBERS OF THE POST OFFICE WHO GAVE THEIR LIVES
IN THE TWO WORLD WARS AND IN SPECIAL MEMORY OF

R Alexander	R Cummins	B Fobbester
H B Allen		M Fobbester
S R Bedwell		J F Govey
R Beech		L A Hook
M Brown		J D Morphew
R J Causley		R W Norman
A R Chapman		J Radford
E Chapman		J Robson
H Chapman		H G Sawkins
B Cheesman		J Taylor
R Durant		E Williams

OPENED ON 18th JUNE 2001 TO CELEBRATE THE 50th ANNIVERSARY OF
THE FOUNDING OF THE POST OFFICE FELLOWSHIP OF REMEMBRANCE

The Garden of Remembrance which was opened in June 2001 to celebrate the 50th Anniversary of
the founding of the Post Office Fellowship of Remembrance:-JRH©

The Hall

Repton was commissioned by Edward Holland in 1830 to build a three-storey house south-east of the village of Dumbleton in the Mock Tudor style which was becoming popular at this time. It was found that designing such a mansion often looked fine in the initial drawings but when put into practice, did not always achieve the desired effect planned for. Dumbleton appears to lack the depth and boldness of the moulding, but when the Temple Guiting ashlar Cotswold stone was new, the house would have looked stunning.

Widworthy Court in Devon, which may have been one of the earlier plans for the Hall at Dumbleton

There were, in fact, two schemes initiated by Repton, and one was similar in design to *Widworthy Court* in Devon. When you look at the present Hall you can see what the original design must have looked like before the later additions and alterations.

An early sketch of Dumbleton Hall showing what the original house would have looked like:-courtesy of 'The Dumbleton Society' & the late Don Caisey© (see colour plate)

Repton's original 1830s house has in fact survived, with the addition of the north wing in the early part of the Twentieth Century. This extension was originally one storey but was later enlarged to match the rest of the house. It was built to accommodate the growing number of staff at the Hall and for extra guest accommodation, but has spoiled what must have been the original symmetry of the mansion.

The main building was originally conceived as a square, with a series of stepped projections and canted by bay windows, which are both beautiful and functional in letting in lots of light and offering fine views from various angles. On the west side the angles of the house are clasped by buttresses, complete with pepper pot finials at roof level. These provide an interesting decorative feature to the roof level in addition to the enormous chimney stacks. The purpose of these separate towers was to give access to the various floors for the servants, without them having to use the main staircase or run into the family or guests.

The octagonal Jacobean ogre-roofed turrets at the outer corners of the building, the servants' staircase and the splendid chimney stacks:-JRH©

116

Inside the house the interior plan, has included large, comfortable well lit rooms arranged around a central top lit hall.

The top lit Hall with its stunning plasterwork, friezes and finials. This is a survival of part of the original house:-JRH©

The drawing room faces south and today occupies the whole of the one side of the house. Originally the eastern section of the Hall formed a separate morning room. The western end of the drawing room leads off from the 60ft conservatory, which today in the present Hall acts as a small conference room.

The beautiful brass work handle and lock cover on the drawing room door:-JRH©

The Drawing Room c1920 & in 2015:- courtesy of the Dumbleton Society and the late Don Caisey collection and Dumbleton Hall Hotel©

A different view of the same room with the magnificent friezes and ceiling decoration probably by George Bankart:-courtesy of Martin Grafton- archivist, the Dumbleton Society and the late Don Caisey©

Detail of the fireplace in the Drawing Room: - courtesy of Mr Martin Grafton-Archivist, the Dumbleton Society and the late Don Caisey©

The Drawing room from the opposite side, with the splendid plasterwork painted and a fine marble fireplace: - courtesy of Martin Grafton-Archivist, the Dumbleton Society and the late Don Caisey©

The present conservatory dates from the late 19th Century and replaced a fully glazed building which was originally part of Repton's original house.

The early conservatory with its glazed roof which is so much more interesting than its modern version. The Conservatory:-courtesy of Mr Martin Grafton and the Dumbleton Hall Hotel©

The Conservatory today, which is not as splendid as when it had its full glass roof:-JRH©

The central room on the west front was the library and today is a charming intimate room with a bar and the original book shelves still in situ.

Early photograph of the library c1920/30: courtesy of Mr Martin Grafton-archivist©

A view of the library and bar in August 2014:-JRH and Dumbleton Hall Hotel©

124

An early view of the library: - courtesy of Mr Martin Grafton-Archivist©

A view of the Billiard Room: - courtesy of the Dumbleton Society and the late Don Caisey©

Today the Billiard Room is a comfortable meeting room and a space for intimate dining

A wedding laid out in the Oak Room: - courtesy of Mr Gavin Dron and the Dumbleton Hall Hotel©

A small study in the north east corner of the house, completes the circuit of rooms. Attached to the northern side of the house is the service wing, originally only two storeys and much smaller and less obtrusive, at that time.

The original square shaped mansion with its distinctive pepper pot finials is clearly seen with the lighter and less attractive north wing, whose stumpy tower does not quite match the original design. The wonderful bay windows are also missing from this extension.

It is interesting to see the fine plastered ceiling in the entrance hall which is likely to have been a possible survival from the original house of the 1830s. Here is a very early photograph of the staircase and the entrance hall, with a large wooden decorated pillar in the middle, which today does not exist.

An early photograph of the front entrance hall looking towards the staircase:-courtesy of Martin Grafton-Archivist, the Dumbleton Society and the late Don Caisey©

The same view of the staircase c1920: courtesy of Martin Grafton-Archivist©

The first floor Landing showing the animal trophies:-courtesy of Martin Grafton-Archivist©

A later view of the entrance hall showing the fine wooden panelling and the magnificent chandelier: - courtesy of Martin Grafton-Archivist©

Two views of the entrance hall, showing the magnificent chandelier, fireplace and decorative plasterwork, which were more than likely part of the original house: - courtesy of Martin Grafton- archivist©

The entrance hall in 2014:-courtesy of the Dumbleton Hall Hotel©

The entrance doors to the present hotel:-JRH©

The magnificent Porte cochere at Dumbleton and cherub on his winged horse in 2014:-JRH©

DUMBLETON HALL, FRONT VIEW, GLOS.

A postcard of Dumbleton Hall c1930:- courtesy of Martin Purches©

Lady Eyres in a magnificent limousine before 1902/5 when the porte cochere was built: - courtesy of
Martin Grafton and the Dumbleton Hall Hotel©

EVM.153 THE LITTLE STAIRCASE, DUMBLETON HALL, NEAR EVESHAM, WORCESTERSHIRE

1ˢᵗ Floor Landing Staircase:-courtesy of Martin Grafton and the Dumbleton Hall Hotel

The same staircase in 2014:-JRH©

The original house interiors were reputed to have included decorative finishes by the Scottish decorator, David Ramsey Hay, and the shutters in the library are indeed stained and grained in a form and style which may signify his work. It is difficult to be absolutely sure of what remains of the original decorative features of the Hall and what has been added later.

David Ramsey FRSE (March 1798, Edinburgh – 10th September 1866) –

was the son of a published poet and also of Robert Burns, Rebekah Carmichael. After her husband had died, David was lucky to have an uncle who stepped in to help educate him. Later he was apprenticed as a painter with the house-painters Gavin Beugo and Robertson in Edinburgh, as was his friend the topographical artist David Roberts. In 1812 he started work for Walter Scott at Abbotsford and in 1850 decorated Holyrood house for Queen Victoria. In the 1920s Queen Mary had these decorative schemes painted over, but the watercolours which were commissioned by Queen Victoria in 1863 give some idea of their appearance.

Abbotsford the home of Sir Walter Scott

The Entrance Hall at Abbotsford

Hay was an advocate of unusual and imitative finishes on his decorative schemes including marbling and graining. He also enjoyed using textured paints to imitate brocade fabrics. From 1828 he developed the theory of colour harmony over six successive editions of his book, 'The Laws of Harmonious Colouring Adapted to Interior Decorations'. In his sixth edition he wrote in detail about his work for Walter Scott at Abbotsford.

With the massive changes to the house interiors in the early twentieth century, it is difficult to be sure what the original decorations looked like, and what is new and which is original. Some of the decorative features which still remain in the plasterwork in the house today may be original. Here are some examples.

In 1902, the Dumbleton estate was purchased by the Eyres-Monsell family who had already been leasing the estate for some years previously. (Kelly's Directory: 1885-1939). Shortly after they had taken on the estate it was decided to embark on a major remodelling of the Hall. The biggest changes to the house were the addition of the entrance vestibule and the 'porte cochere' and also the enormous extension to the north wing to provide extra bedrooms and staff accommodation.

New entrance door and the vestibule door leading into the main entrance hall in 2014:-JRH©

The enormous north wing extension which was originally one storey but then was extended to three:-
JRH©

The architect for the new remodelling was probably Sidney Kitson (of Bedford) and Kitson of Leeds, who were known to have designed buildings for the estate during this period of change. From the changes which took place it does not look as if the new architects had very much sympathy with the symmetry of the original house. They have tried to incorporate the original pepper pot towers finials but the effort is stumpy and the lack of the fine bay windows make this extension more of an office block outline without the fine bay windows of the original.

The work of the 1902-5 redecorations included a complete change to the interior, although the fine entrance hall plaster ceiling was left in its original form. The fine wooden panelling here has been painted white, which seems a great pity, but makes the large area much lighter. The original ceiling is difficult to accurately date but more than likely is the work of David Ramsey Hay or even Alexander Roos as this appears in his style:

The fine plasterwork ceiling of the entrance hall:-JRH©

In the drawing room the plasterwork is much finer and more delicate in style and includes its deep plaster frieze of base relief. This example of the *Art Nouveau* style depicts trees, birds and figures with a matching ceiling of various flowers in lozenges.

The splendid plastered ceiling in the drawing room showing the various lozenges with their plants and flowers:-JRH©

Part of the splendid plasterwork frieze at Dumbleton, once painted or stained. It was probably the work of George Percy Bankart:-JRH©

Much of Kitson's plasterwork elsewhere was executed by George Bankart, and so it is most likely that he was also involved here, although there are no firm accounts or records to confirm this.

George Percy Bankart – 1866-1929

George Percy Bankart. This is a family photograph by kind consent of his great granddaughter Marguerite Salter©

George was born in Leicester and his father also called George (1831-1917) was born in Bradford. He was a merchant and an insurance broker of Swiss descent. George attended the Wyggeston Grammar School and the Leicester School of Art (1845-92) where he met Ernest Gimson (1864-1919). Through Grimson, George was introduced to William Morris and a number of other leading architects and craftsmen including Mervyn McCartney, Sydney Barnsley and W. R. Lethaby, all active in the style of the Arts and Crafts Movement which was popular at this time.

Bankart was appointed instructor in architecture and modelling at the Leicester School of Art in 1897. He had begun to develop an interest in lead work and also decorative plastering.

Around 1899 Bankart moved from Leicester to Bromsgrove and for the next seven years worked at the Bromsgrove Guild with Henry Ludlow expanding the decorative plasterwork and lead shops. Among the completed commissions that Bankart undertook at this time was the Great Hall of the London Naval College in (1903-4).

The ceiling of the Great Naval College in London under repair in the 1950s

In 1906 he left the Bromsgrove Guild and set up his own independent business in Baldwin's Gardens, Gray's Inn Road, London. In 1910 it was reported that Bankart had merged his business with the longstanding firm of Jacksons. George published a number of books on plastering including '*The Art of the Plasterer: an account of the decorative development of the craft' in 1908. (Information for this biography* came from '*Mr George Bankart and his work*', Grey Wornum, The Architect's Journal, 12th October 1927.)

The former dining room has a fine white marble chimney piece of c1740, which was probably brought into the Hall at this time. It is a splendid part of this room's decorations in the present hotel.

The fine marble fireplace in the former dining room at Dumbleton Hall Hotel:-JRH©

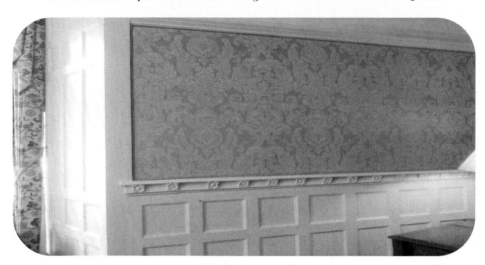

The former dining room with its painted panelling and decorative patterns:-JRH©

Here is another fine plasterwork ceiling which is a continuation of the dining room design into a later small sitting room and now a comfortable bar in the present hotel:-JRH©

In the 1950s, like so many country houses, Dumbleton suffered from high government taxation which made it difficult to live in such a large house. Staff was expensive, salaries had risen and after the 2nd World War not many people wished to go into low paid domestic service.

The government had taken over many of the finer country houses at the start of the war, and on its conclusion the families returned to find their homes in a terrible state which they could not afford to repair or pay for. There was some government compensation but many families did not get this or it was not enough to pay for what was needed. Many were subsequently demolished or sold to developers who either demolished the houses or sold off what they could or they were turned into schools or divided up into flats and apartments.

In the 1950s Dumbleton was in this position and the family found that supporting the enormous house, with servants and staff becoming scarce, and those who could be employed demanding higher salaries was very difficult. Families had become smaller anyway and living in such a large house was no longer practical. In 1959, Dumbleton, which could have easily been demolished, was sold instead to the Post Office Fellowship of Remembrance as a living memorial to those Post Office servicemen who had lost their lives or been severely injured in both the First and the Second World Wars. Initially, the Hall was used as a quiet retreat for convalescence and quiet holidays for the post office staff and later it was opened to the general public as a hotel. The Dumbleton Estate was later sold to Lord Hambro.

* *

1ˢᵗ Earl Somers –Romney:-courtesy of the Eastnor Castle Collection©

Edward Holland:-courtesy of the 'University of Agriculture,' Cirencester©

The Gold Medals Awarded for the best Student who gained the Diploma in Estate Management: - courtesy of Lorna Parker (archivist) & the 'University of Agriculture' in Cirencester©

(III)

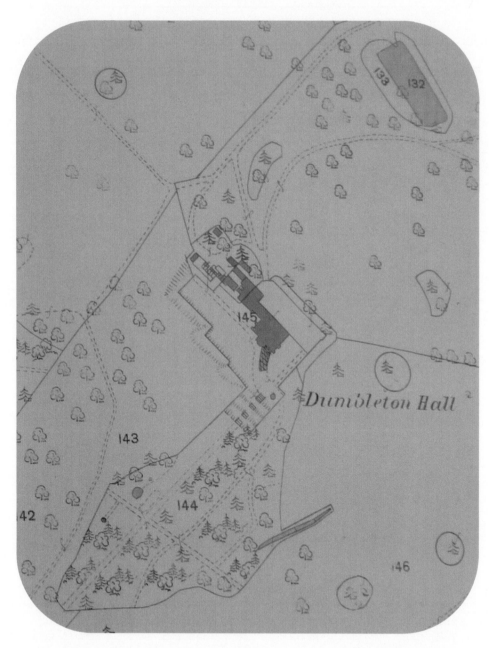

The OS Map of Dumbleton Hall for 1883:- courtesy of OS and to Sue Campbell©

Mrs Eyres at Dumbleton c1900 before the building of the 'porte-cochere':-
courtesy of the Dumbleton Society & the late Don Caisey©

Chatsworth House - Derbyshire

Charles Darwin as a child

Early Sketch of Dumbleton Hall: - courtesy of the 'Dumbleton Society' & the late Don Caisey©

Dumbleton Hall in August 2014:- courtesy of JRH©

Dumbleton Hall from the west- showing the original house and the later north extension in summer 2014:-JRH©

*Dumbleton facing west with the more formal gardens in c1923/4:-courtesy of Mr
Martin Grafton-Archivist©*

Dumbleton Hall in the Snow: courtesy of Matt Davis-Photographer©

Kathleen Mary Ferrier 1912-1953 & the Memorial piano at Dumbleton Hall

Kathleen Ferrier travelled to sing in New York on board the 'Queen Mary' the 'Queen Elizabeth' and the 'R.M.S. Mauretania'.

*A Women's Land Army Poster from World War 2 - Dumbleton was a Land Girl
Hostel from 1943 to 1947.*

Early view of the Hall and the gardens in their heyday:-courtesy of the Dumbleton Society & the late Don Caisey©

Early photograph of the Drawing Room at Dumbleton Hall:-courtesy of the Dumbleton Society and the late Don Caisey©

Patrick and Joan Fermor's Greek home at Kalamitsi in 2014

Bolton Meredith Eyres-Monsell, I *Viscount Monsell, GBE, PC – 1881-1969:-courtesy of the National Portrait Gallery, London ©*

The Oak Lounge made ready for a wedding: - courtesy of Mr Martin Grafton, Mr Simon Kelly, the manager Mr Gavin Dron and the Dumbleton Hotel©

Friars Carse in Scotland and Waterhead on Coniston Water, Cumbria which are Post Office Fellowship of Remembrance Homes: courtesy of Mr Martin Grafton©

The Monsell Memorial Window in St Olave's Church, Hart Street, London: - Photograph by Phil Manning Image© St Olave Church, Hart Street, London PCC 2015 by permission.

Dumbleton Hall in the spring:-courtesy of Mr Simon Kelly and the Dumbleton Hall Hotel©

(XXIII)

A Wedding at Dumbleton Hall: - courtesy of Mr Gavin Dron, Mr Simon Kelly and the Dumbleton Hall Hotel©

(XXIV)

Examples of the beautifully painted illuminated letters for the Post Office Memorial Books

Postcard of Dumbleton Hall showing the fine conservatory and the layout of the grounds:-courtesy of Mr Martin Purches©

H. G. Watkins

From an oil-painting by his F

A painting of 'Gino Watkins' by his Father – 29th January 1907 – 20th August 1932 –aged 25 years

(XXVII)

Chapter Five: The Eyres-Monsell Family & Additions to the Hall

In 1875 **Henry William Eyres** leased the Dumbleton estate, which was subsequently bought by his family, as Edward Holland's will had left his eldest son with insufficient means to maintain the estate. By 1880 the Eyres family bought the estate outright and in this year Henry also married **Caroline Isabel Sharp** on the 20th October. Sadly Henry was to enjoy the company of his new wife and his new home for only a short time for in the following April while on a visit to Naples he died, leaving a pregnant wife. Her daughter **Caroline Mary Sybil** was born in the following August.

The Eyres family fortune had been built up by **Samuel Eyres** a Yorkshire wool merchant: and from this business sufficient funds were available for Henry William to purchase the Dumbleton estate. An article appeared in the *Leeds Times* which spoke of Samuel Eyres's demise in January 1868:

'*A Leeds Millionaire has departed this life during the past week. Mr. Samuel Eyres had for a number of years been the principal member of the well known firm of William Eyres & Sons, woollen manufacturers and merchants, of Leeds and Armley, and the career of his house has of late been almost exceptionally successful. This was partly owing to the business application of the deceased, and partly to the extreme penuriousness which marked his personal expenditure, and which characterized all his business transactions in which he was engaged. He could drive a very hard bargain in commercial matters, and as a consequence many needy clothiers went to him to dispose of their goods, inasmuch as they were certain of obtaining their cash when the negotiation was concluded. Some years ago he used to attend the German wool fairs, and on one occasion it is related, he bought up all the raw material shown in the market, a little transaction which slightly disturbed the equanimity of the stolid burghers. We do not find that he ever took an active share in either politics or social questions, his peculiar bent and disposition, being to acquire wealth, which he succeeded in accumulating to the extent, it is rumoured, of above a million and a half. It was stated in Leeds yesterday that Mr. Eyres left the sum of £10,000 to the New Infirmary, and we should not say we should be delighted to find that the story is correct. The deceased, who is in his 74th year, was seized with a bronchial attack last Friday and died from the effects on Tuesday morning. His remains will be interred at Armley Church this (Saturday) morning.*'

St Bartholomew's Armley Church. It is interesting to note that when the Viscountess Eyres-Monsell had come of age, she had been given the money to complete the tower of this Church. What a birthday present ! This was to mark her association with her great-grandfather and with Armley.

* *

In 1881 Henry's widow was pregnant with his daughter, Caroline Mary Sybil Eyres. 'Sybil' she was always called, married Bolton Meredith Monsell in 1904, who changed his surname to Eyres-Monsell.

After the death of her father Caroline Mary Sybil must have rented Dumbleton Hall, as the census for 1901 does not show her family living there – they seemed to have rented Dumbleton to a Widow called Maria Sharp.

Dumbleton Census for 1901

Name	Age	Position	Married	Born
Maria Sharp	73	Head - widow	Widow	Wortley, Yorkshire
Clara B. Cowan	56	Visitor	Widow	London
Arthur H. Sharp	39	Brother – Barrister at Law- Retired	Widower	Bagley, Yorkshire
Maud H. W. Sharp	7	Niece		London
Margaret F. Laurie	22	Governess	unmarried	Southampton Hants
Robert Rooney	42	Butler	unmarried	Dorchester, Dorset
Joseph H. Higgs	20	Footman	unmarried	Kenilworth, Warwickshire
Charles H. Frampton	15	Page Boy	unmarried	Norwood, Surrey
Elizabeth White	41	Cook	unmarried	Newbury, Berkshire
Rose Larner	23	Housemaid	unmarried	Dumbleton, Glos
Priscilla Hawkins	39	Housemaid	unmarried	Dumbleton, Gloucestershire
Lydia Hine	22	Housemaid	unmarried	Lincoln

Martha Belcher	24	Parlour Maid	unmarried	Kinsham, Worcestershire
Edith Weaver	20	Kitchen Maid	unmarried	Dumbleton, Gloucestershire

It is interesting to note that there were no Nurses as in the previous census, but a Governess for most likely Maud Sharp's niece who was 7 at this time. All the servants are also unmarried and most of them were born some distance away from Dumbleton. The pageboy was only 15 and had come from Surrey, so it was unlikely he saw very much of his family while he was working at Dumbleton, but after the Eyres-Monsell's moved in a year or so later, we are not sure if this or some of this staff remained, or new staff were taken on.

It looks as if Sybil knew Maria Sharp, as they both appear on the 1891 Census staying at Whitwell on the Isle of Wight. On the Census is listed *Caroline S. Eyres as head a widow with her daughter aged 9. Maria Sharpe is listed as her mother and Arthur Sharp her brother, and they both appear on the 1901 Census for Dumbleton. Maud is the daughter with a niece Beatrice and there is a governess, Evelyn James who is 24 and single.*

* *

Bolton Meredith Eyres - Monsell, 1ˢᵗ Viscount Monsell, GBE, PC – 1881-1969 was a British Conservative Party politician. He took up politics after he married Sybil Eyres and left the Navy. He served as *Chief Whip* from 1923 until 1931 and then as *First Lord of the Admiralty* in the 1930s in the run up to the Second World War and the rise of Hitler in Germany.

Bolton Meredith Eyres-Monsell: - courtesy of the National Portrait Gallery, London©

His Anglo-Irish Ascendancy family were a branch of the Monsells of Tervoe, who had first settled in County Limerick, Ireland in the 17ᵗʰ Century.

His father was an army officer and then became the Chief Constable of the Metropolitan Police from 1886 until 1910. His mother was Mary Beverley Ogle (died 1929), and was the 2nd daughter of General Sir Edmund Ogle, 6ᵗʰ Baronet; Monsell was the youngest of their two sons in a family of six children.

His schooling included a prep school at *Stubbington House* in Fareham, and his family decided for him a career in the Royal Navy, entering *HMS. Britannia* as a cadet in 1894.

Stubbington House School - was founded in 1841 as a boys' preparatory school, originally located in the Hampshire village of Stubbington, around 1 mile (1.6 km) from the Solent. Stubbington House School was known by the soubriquet "*the cradle of the Navy*". The school was relocated to Ascot in 1962, merging with *Earleywood School*, and it closed in 1997.)

A view of what remains of the Stubbington Prep School that Lord Monsell attended. This image was taken in 1965. The school appears to be a ruin.

HMS Britannia training cadets in 1895

He first went to sea as a midshipman in 1896 and specialised as a Torpedo Lieutenant in 1903. His marriage the following year to an heiress brought his naval career to an end and gave him the opportunity to move his career into politics. This move would see him have the chance to witness and take a role in some of the major decisions of the early Twentieth Century, and those grim years of the Great Depression and the Rise of Hitler and the Nazi Party in Germany.

His marriage on the 3rd December 1904 was to Caroline Mary Sybil Eyres (1881-1959), who was the only child of Henry William Eyres of **Dumbleton Hall,** near Evesham in Worcestershire.

* *

In 1910 an interesting extract from the *Cheltenham Chronicle* – 11th June 1910 mentions Mrs Eyres-Monsell:

'Worcestershire and Hereford Show, Mrs Eyres-Monsell of Dumbleton was awarded 4 prizes for Jersey Cattle.'

Jersey Cattle at Dumbleton:-courtesy of the Dumbleton Society and the late Don Caisey©

She is mentioned again in October 1915 in the *Birmingham Post:*

'By kind permission of Mrs Eyres-Monsell a concert will be given at Dumbleton Hall on Thursday October 21ˢᵗ at 3 o' clock in aid of the British Red Cross. Tickets (including tea) 10/6 and 5/-.'

An interesting article appeared in '*The Listening Post*' the Newsletter of the *Western Front Association* Worcestershire and Hereford Branch in the August 2013 edition entitled '*The Lady in the Lifeboat*' by Sam Eedle and Brian Hill. I have sorted their permission to use part of their article for this book.

While Eyres-Monsell was on duty in the Royal Navy on operations in the eastern Mediterranean in 1915, his wife set sail on the 11,000 ton Japanese liner the '*Yasaka Maru*' en route via Egypt.

The Japanese liner 'Yasaka Maru'

The ship was ornately decorated in the Japanese style and had a capacity for 500 passengers but on this particular voyage only had 51 men, 54 women, 15 children and the crew on board. Lady Sybil Eyres-Monsell was accompanied by her lady's maid, the 44 year old Isabel Cameron from Rosshire in Scotland. Why Lady Eyres-Monsell was travelling on the liner is a mystery but on December 21st 1915, just sixty miles north of the coast of Egypt, the liner sailed into the path of the German submarine U38 which was commanded by Captain Max Valentiner, who with his submarine had already proved a problem in the Mediterranean. Mrs Eyres-Monsell takes up the events of that day in a letter which was later published in the 'Upton News' on January 22nd 1916.

'MRS EYRES-MONSELL'S ADVENTURE.

EXPERIENCED ON A TORPEDOED LINER.'

'Mrs Eyres-Monsell, wife of our gallant and popular member, has happily, suffered no ill effects from her exciting experiences when the Japanese liner, 'Yasaka Maru,' was sunk without warning by an enemy submarine on the journey to Port Said on December 21. In the following letter home she gives an entertaining account of her experiences:

Shepherd's Hotel, Cairo   Friday, December 24th 1915

"Now I have so much to tell you that I don't know where to begin. First, will you tell everyone who sent out parcels by me that I regret they are all at the bottom of the sea? It's a funny sensation not even possessing a toothbrush. However, I am now the happy owner of a black and white coat and skirt and a black hat – so I'm getting on.

155

Lady Sybil Eyres-Monsell – this photograph appeared on the front cover of 'The Ladies Field' magazine in September 1913.

Now I will tell you all about the shipwreck! It happened at about 2.45 in the afternoon. I was dressed in my old brown tweed and my little purple velvet hat, as we did not expect to get in till after dinner and I was going to make myself respectable later. I had just gone down to my cabin and was discussing one or two things with Cameron, when there came this violent bang which shook the whole ship. Cameron remarked, 'There now, there's that submarine' and started hastily putting things into her bag! I got down the lifebelts and put one on and my big coat. I remembered I'd left my rug on my chair on deck, so I collected that on the way up and went to the top deck to the boats. Just when the bang came I don't think I felt frightened; it was just a sort of hopeless feeling that everything one possessed must be lost.

When I got into bed I found my tongue and throat so dry that I could hardly swallow – a form of fright, I suppose. The first boat was just being lowered and was very crowded, so Mrs Sutherland called out to me to come along to the next, which was just being got out, so we fell in among oars and spare, etc., everyone on the top of everyone else, and we were lowered into the water – most unpleasant, as one thought the boat might be swamped. Our boat wasn't a bit full fortunately, and we got away from the ship all right;

then the Japs didn't want to go too far away in case people were still left on board and we could rescue them. However, soon the Captain was seen in a boat, and so they knew everyone was off the ship and we got right away from it as well as we could.

The U38 commanded by Christian August Max Ahlmann Valentiner

It was all very lucky for us really, if it had to happen, as she was hit fairly forward, and she didn't go on one side at all; when we were first in the boat then she seemed to be tilted up a little, while the bows were rather further in the water than usual. Then gradually the bows went down and down, and then half of her was in the water and the other half standing straight and up out of the water with clouds of black smoke coming out, then there was an explosion – not a very big one – and finish; nothing of the great ship one had been living in half an hour before except a few spars and wreckage floating about. I think it was the most horrible thing I've seen in my life.

After that we collected round the Captain's boat and he made some of the people get out of the crowded boats into the emptier ones, put an officer in charge of each and men of the crew who could row and put up sails, etc., and tied all the boats together in a long line so as to keep them all under his eye. Then he told us that he's 'wirelessed' to Port Said at once for help and that they had answered and were sending a rescue ship.

There was no wind and no rain – quite a peaceful day, only a bit of a swell and I'm afraid lots of people were ill. I never felt a bit bad, though we lopped about till about 12.30 (night). It was quite warm all night and I never wanted my thick coat or my rug; in fact a funny little Indian man spent the night wrapped in the rug, as he'd removed his thick outer garments, thinking he was most likely going into the sea, and another woman had my coat as a pillow, as she attempted to sleep and I couldn't. At about 5 o'clock we had two ship's biscuits given out all round, and that was all I had to eat (one of them) from one o' clock *one day till 10.30 the next morning, but I never felt hungry, thirsty or sleepy all the time. For a little bit in the small boat I had a bad head, so I ate a bit of biscuit and felt better. We were 25 in our boat. Presently, after some hours, we saw a light – great excitement! Lights were put up at some mastheads and red flares burnt, but nothing came of it. Then a little later there was another one, and that ship came quite close, but she was only a small passenger ship, and of course frightened of the submarine, but when she heard we were expecting a rescue ship she went on.*

I forgot to tell you that we saw the periscope of the submarine quite plainly waiting about near the boats until they were quite sure the ship was going to sink! It was a lovely moonlight night, and we looked just like a little fishing fleet bobbing up and down with the sails flapping. At last, about 12.30; there came along a small black boat with no lights, and rolling most unpleasantly – the Rescue Ship – great excitement and much applause from all the Japs. Then we had to get on board, with our boats rolling one way and the ship rolling the other, and she was so low that there was no ladder or anything of that sort, so it was just a case of being hauled over the sides by two men and arriving on board head first. It was a very small sort of French tug or old gunboat, with a gun on board, so there wasn't much room, and everyone sat or lay about anywhere. Cameron and I sat on some oil tins, and if for one moment one stood up without holding on one knocked into everyone anywhere near with great violence because she rolled so!

People of course were dressed anyhow, half of them hadn't any hats on. One women was changing her dress, so just had a fur coat on top of her petticoat, and there were several women with small babies and no nurse or anyone with them. It must have been awful for them. Many of them had lost all they possessed – their money, and hadn't a penny of money.

Our boats were tied on behind and of course with such a heavy load we took ages getting in, and didn't arrive till about 10 o'clock, and it was a very hot sunny day, and of course one looked particularly awful by daylight. Of course we felt very superior being taken on shore by three sailors, and Alec and Freddy Noble were so splendid. They'd both been up all night with Bobby; the wireless got in at three o'clock that we'd been torpedoed, but they knew nothing more – whether anyone had been rescued, etc., until 3 a.m. Poor Bobby arrived at Port Said at 4 o'clock very cheery, and they had to tell him the ship had been torpedoed an hour before, but they knew nothing more at all, so you can imagine what a night he had.

Of course I went out at once and bought a few necessary garments. I went to bed in the afternoon, but couldn't sleep for very long. Thursday we came on here, of course, everything most interesting for me; along the canal to Ismailia, which is quite an attractive little place, and then straight across; first of all a bit of the desert, and then the delta of the Nile, which of course, has gone through all this wonderful scheme of irrigation. I felt all the time that I was looking at a scene out of a play. I couldn't really believe I was seeing genuine camels, Arabs riding on the little donkeys, the flat-roofed houses, and palm trees. The place swarms with soldiers.'

We can only guess at why Sybil was travelling in such a dangerous place, but presumably to be close to her husband in Egypt. He was later awarded the Order of the Nile, by the Sultan of Egypt, and also mentioned in Dispatches.

Sybil was involved in war related work and was awarded the CBE (LG 7-6-1918), as *'Donor and Administrator, Annex to King Edward VII's Hospital at 17 Grosvenor Crescent, in London, then known as the King Edward VII's Hospital for Officers.'*

The badge worn by Commanders (CBE), Knight Commanders (KBE), & Dame Commanders (DBE) with military ribbon

King Edward VII'th Hospital for Officers- used today by the Royal Family

As well as living at Dumbleton at this time, Sybil and her husband leased *104 Eaton Square* in London (LG 18-7-1922). The Eyres-Monsells also had a house at *No. 19 Belgrave Square*. When Lord Monsell was Chief Whip he would have had the use of No. 12 Downing Street also.

The north side of Eaton Square- the Government were established here from 1940-44

No. 12 is part of the darker brick buildings on Downing Street- the office and residence of the Chief Whip

19 Belgrave Square in March 2015:-JRH©

104 Eaton Square in March 2015:-JRH©

The submarine U38 which had caused Lady Sybil so much trouble was commanded by *Christian August Max Ahlmann Valentiner*, which at the time was on a devastating two month patrol of the Mediterranean in late 1915.

Christian August Max Ahlmann Valentiner

During this time he was responsible for the sinking of over 23 ships, both warships and merchant ships. Eighteen were sunk between November 3rd and December 30th 1915, including the *'Yasaka Maru'* and the British liner *'Persia'*. (I would like to acknowledge Mr Brian Hill for finding this letter and Mr Sam Eedle for his article.)

Valentiner was listed after the war as a war criminal by the British Authorities. He died in 1949 in Sonderborg, Denmark.

The loss of the British liner 'Persia'

Lady Sybil Eyres-Monsell was buried at Dumbleton in St Peter's Churchyard close to the grave of her mother *Caroline Isabel Eyres* who like her daughter had spent many years of her life at Dumbleton Hall and played an active role in the village and on the estate here.

The gravestone in St Peter's Churchyard of Viscountess Eyres-Monsell. The inscription reads: '*Born 1881 Died 1959 - In loving Memory of Caroline Mary Sybil Eyres Viscountess Monsell.* The cross is the grave of her mother.

The inscription reads: Caroline Isabel Eyres who passed away December 14th 1921

In January 1910, Lord Monsell became the Conservative MP for Evesham his local town and the following year the Chief Whip at the suggestion of Bonar Law.

Andrew Bonar Law 1858-1923, commonly known as 'Bonar' was a Conservative Party statesman and Prime Minister.

It is interesting at this point to look at the 1911 Census for Dumbleton and who was living at the Hall and those in the village connected with the Hall at this time.

The Stables, Dumbleton:

William Garvin, Widower Age 45 – Coachman plus 3 children and his cousin who was his housekeeper

The Lodge, Dumbleton:

Walter Sallis 43, Single Gardener, Domestic, plus his widowed mother, his sister and a servant

New Lodge, Dumbleton:

George Edward Pritchard, Married Age 50, Gardener, Domestic plus wife and boarder

The Palaces, Dumbleton:

Herbert Boddy, Married, Age 31, Gamekeeper Plus wife and child

Dumbleton Village:

Frank Fellows , Married, Age 27 Chauffeur (Domestic)

Plus wife and 2 children

Dumbleton Hall:

Bolton Eyres Monsell, 30 Married Lieut RN MP Born Hants Hamble, Yorks

Plus:

Lady's Maid

4 Housemaids

Kitchen Maid

Scullery Maid

2 Footmen

Electric Light Assistant

Only 1 of the servants listed in the house was local.

Bolton Eyres-Monsell declared that the Hall had 50 rooms. Neither of the two children of the family was at home when the census was taken.

During the First World War, Lord Monsell again served as a Royal Navy officer, achieving the rank of Commander and was awarded the '*Order of the Nile*' by the Sultan of Egypt. (The Order of the Nile is Egypt's highest state honour. The award was instituted by Sultan Hussein Kamel in 1915 for exceptional services to the nation. It was reconstituted under the Arab Republic of Egypt in 1953.)

The Order of the Nile

He was **Civil Lord of the Admiralty** from April 1921 to October 1922; then **Parliamentary and Financial Secretary to the Admiralty** until May 1923, **Parliamentary Secretary to the Treasury** from July 1923 to January 1924 and again from November 1924 to June 1929 and from September 1931 to November 1931. He became **First Lord of the Admiralty** in 1931, retaining the office in government until 1936.

Viscount Monsell:-courtesy of the NPG in London©

He was on good terms with **Stanley Baldwin** who was the MP for the local Bewdley constituency with other Conservative anti-coalitionists and he was chosen as Chief Whip when Stanley Baldwin became leader of the Conservative Party. He became a **Privy Councillor** on July 7th 1923 and he took over the position of **Chief Whip** on 25th July 1923.

(Monsell served as Chief Whip for eight years and was always considered by many politicians to be one of the most successful holders of the office. The **Chief Whip** is a political office in some legislatures assigned to an elected member whose task is to administer the whipping system that ensures that members of the party attend and vote as the party leadership desires.)

He was said to possess great charm and impeccable manners, and was both amusing and intelligent. It was said of him that he was the *'best dressed man in the House of Commons'*.

Monsell was strikingly handsome, cultivated and sociable and he enjoyed socialising with the 'smart set of the time'. He enjoyed yachting and holidays with friends, especially those in the Mediterranean.

He also loved his country life, where shooting was especially enjoyed. He invited down to **Dumbleton**, only those who could shoot well.

Around c1926, there were many parties and shoots at **Dumbleton.** In 2002 Mr Grafton who was researching Dumbleton at this time received a letter from *Diana Moseley,* one of the *Mitford Sisters* who mentions her brother Tom and herself visiting the Hall for tennis parties. She states they had great fun but did not meet Lord Monsell on the visits. Judging by the reputation these sisters and their friends gained, it was not surprising that Lord Monsell was not at home when the *'high jinks'* were being enacted at his country house.

Early family photograph of the Mitford family

The Mitford Family was a minor aristocratic family whose main family seat was at Mitford, in Northumberland, although they lived later quite close to Dumbleton at Batsford near Moreton-in-Marsh. The sisters became particularly celebrated and at times scandalous for their lives and their marriages.

When they would have visited Dumbleton they would have been young teenagers and from all reports full of fun. They must have had great times at the hall. Lord Monsell would not have been there during their visits to the younger members of his family. He did have a swimming pool built at the Hall, which today is a small secluded garden.

The garden which today has replaced the secluded swimming pool where the young guests to the Hall could bathe

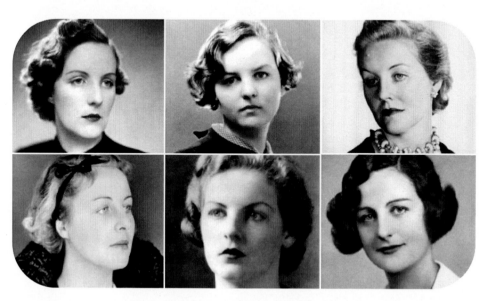

Six of the famous and beautiful Mitford sisters

The lives of the Mitford sisters were the talk of the country and they all had interesting and very varied lives. As young girls they visited Dumbleton as guests of Lady Eyres-Monsell and her children.

The Hon Nancy Mitford (1904-1973), was the eldest of the sisters and later married Peter Rodd and had a long-standing relationship with French Statesman Gaston Palewski. She lived in France for much of her adult life. She was a writer and wrote about historical figures such as her book on the 'Sun King –Louis XIV'. Her novels were well known and included '*Love in a Cold Climate*' and '*The Pursuit of Love*'.

The Hon Nancy Mitford 1904-1973

The second sister the **Hon Pamela Mitford (1907-1994),** married and later divorced the millionaire physicist Derek Jackson. *John Betjeman,* who was also a frequent visitor to **Dumbleton,** was for a time in love with her, and referred to her as the '*Rural Mitford*'. After her divorce she spent the remainder of her life as the companion of *Giuditta Tommasi,* an Italian horsewoman.

The Hon Pamela Mitford 1904-1973:- courtesy of the National Portrait Gallery (1936) ©

The Mitford sisters' brother **Thomas (1909-1945)** was educated at Eton, the lover of James Lees-Milne and the regular lover of Tilly Losch during her marriage to Edward James. Thomas died as a soldier in Burma. According to Jessica's letters, he unofficially supported British fascism and was stationed in Burma after refusing to fight in Europe during the war. Tom was a great friend of Viscount Monsell's son Graham and would have been invited to **Dumbleton** on a number of occasions.

Thomas Mitford 1909-1945

The third sister was the **Hon Diana Mitford (1910-2003)** who married the aristocrat and writer *Bryan Walter Guiness* in the 1929 society wedding of the year. She later left him causing a national scandal (1933) for the British fascist leader *Sir Oswald Mosley*. She was during the Second World was imprisoned in Holloway Prison and in fact never gave up her belief in fascism or her affection for Adolf Hitler. She was the mother of Max Mosley.

Diana Mitford 1910-2003 (later Lady Mosley):- Bassano©

Diana Mitford 1910-2003 at the 1936 Nuremburg Rally

The fourth sister the **Hon Unity Valkyrie Mitford (1914-1948)**, nicknamed '*Bobo*' or '*Boud*' by her siblings. She was famous for her adulation and friendship with Hitler. She later shot herself in the head when Britain declared war on Germany in 1939. She survived her suicide attempt but later died of pneumococcal meningitis at West Cottage Hospital, in Oban, Scotland.

Unity was said to have been a close friend of Hitler

Unity Mitford:-courtesy of the National Portrait Gallery©

The Hon Jessica Mitford (1917-1996) was the fifth sister, she was often known as *'Decca'*. She eloped with *Esmond Romilly* to the *Spanish Civil War* and later spent most of her life in the United States of America. Two years after Esmond was killed in the Second World War she married *Robert Treuhaft* who worked for the American Government. Jessica was a member of the *American Communist Party* until 1958. She wrote several books, including a book about the American funeral business in the *'American Way of Death'* (1963).

Jessica Mitford 1917-1996

The last Mitford sister, the **Hon Deborah Mitford (1920-2014)**, being the youngest probably never accompanied some of her sisters to Dumbleton but would have probably visited the Hall later. She married *Andrew Cavendish* who became the *Duke of Devonshire* and with him turned his ancestral home, *Chatsworth House* into one of Britain's most successful stately homes. She also wrote several books. She was a lifelong friend of Patrick Leigh Fermor, whom she had met through Joan Eyres-Monsell, who later married Patrick. In her '*Tearing Haste Letters*' she had probably the closest links with the family and with Dumbleton.

Deborah Vivien Cavendish (nee Freeman-Mitford) Duchess of Devonshire:-courtesy of the National Portrait Gallery, London©

175

John Betjeman with his family and later in life: - courtesy of the National Portrait Gallery©

John Betjeman while at Magdalen College, Oxford where he studied under C. S. Lewis. He was probably about the age he would have been visiting Dumbleton when he was in love with Pamela Mitford

Sir John Betjeman – 1906-1984 was an English poet, broadcaster and popular writer who from 1972 until his death was Poet Laureate.

He was very interested and impressed by the architecture of the Victorians and after seeing many fine buildings being either neglected or demolished founded the *Victorian Society.*

He studied at *Magdalen College* in Oxford under the young *C.S. Lewis* whom he did not get on with very well. As well as becoming the *Poet Laureate* in 1972, he became the first *Knight Bachelor.* He had his own unique style of writing and his poems became extremely popular to all classes and ages of people. He began his recording career in the 1970s when he brought out some of his collections of poetry and put them to music which became very popular. The four albums on Charisma Records included *'Banana Blush'* (1974) and *'Late Flowering Love'* (1974)

Betjeman wrote a nonsense poem in which *Alan Pryce-Jones* (known as 'Boggins') and *Sir Bolton Eyres-Monsell* both figure:

"Dumbleton"

Dumbleton, Dumbleton the ruin by the lake,
Where Boggins & Sir Bolton fought a duel for thy sake;
Dumbleton, Dumbleton, the Gothic arch that leads
Thro' the silver vestibule to where Sir Bolton feeds.
The groaning of the golden plate,
The Sickly social shame;
Oh heirs of Dumbleton! The Monsell is thy name!"

Betjeman also wrote in a mock Longfellow style later used in *'Longfellow's Visit to Venice',* which begins:

"Not so far from Evesham's city on a woody hillside green
Stands an ancient stonebuilt mansion-nothing modern to be seen,
Not a farmhouse, not a homestead, only trees on either hand
Billowing like heaps of cushions on the sofa of the land...'

John Betjeman Uncollected **Poems** in 1982.

John Betjeman at Dumbleton Hall in 1933. Referring to his new book, '*Ghastly Good Taste*', he captioned this picture: 'The author – an example of good taste if ever there was one'.

* *

Mrs Susan Casey has kindly sent me some of her memories of Dumbleton Hall when she was a girl and used to visit her Grandmother Lady Sybil Eyres-Monsell before the Hall was sold to the Post Office Fellowship of Remembrance in 1959. Mrs Casey was 18 at this time. Her mother was Diana, the oldest daughter of Bolton and Sybil Eyres-Monsell. She wrote to me concerning her family links with John Betjeman:

'*I know that my Aunt Joan, my mother's sister, was a friend of John Betjeman. I was told that in John Betjeman's poem 'Dumbleton Hall' "Stopped, I deem to steal some kisses from the daughter of the Hall" and "...Sir Bolton standing by her... his lovely daughter welcomes every author-guest" was about Joan. Joan certainly knew the Mitfords.*'

I have included this fascinating account of life at Dumbleton when it was a family home which Mrs Susan Casey has kindly written for me:

VISITS TO DUMBLETON HALL

I saw a great deal of my mother's family. We used to stay with my grandmother at Dumbleton Hall two or three times a year. It was a couple of hours' drive from Market Overton to Dumbleton and my father and mother took turns driving, but my father always took over the wheel at The Lodge to drive up to the house. We used to greet our grandmother in the hall and then, weather permitting, we dashed for the swing under the large cedar tree, to the boat on the lake or the lovely grey rocking horse in the conservatory. Then it was to the kitchen to visit Elsie, the cook.

Most days we four children spent as much time as we could rowing the boat from where it was usually tied up by the small waterfall which brought the water coming down from the Dumbleton Hills into the lake, to the end of the lake nearer the house where the water again fell as a small waterfall, and then disappeared underground to come up again in the pond in the park. We would take turns rowing around and sometimes landing on the couple of small islands, and rowing up and down the lake.

My grandmother took us, or arranged for us to be taken, annually to Cheltenham Races for one of their January meetings, and to Badminton Horse Trials in the Easter Holidays. Anna, Bridget and I also went to an Eight to Eighty dance held at the Lygon Arms in Broadway. Sometimes we were also taken shopping at Cavendish House in Cheltenham.

At Dumbleton, we saw sometimes my Uncle Graham, my mother's older brother, and her younger sisters, my Aunt Joan, and Aunt Patricia. Uncle Graham has been almost good enough to be a concert pianist and we had to be quiet when he was playing the piano in the drawing room. This room also contained a ping-pong table and we four children had a wonderful time playing. There were walks around the village and up to the Dumbleton woods where, in their season, wild daffodils grew in profusion and cuckoos called. There was a swimming pool in the garden where we swam with the many frogs who lived in it. Also croquet would be set up on the lawn for us and the grown-ups. My grandmother also always had a jigsaw puzzle on the go.

We ate breakfast, lunch and dinner in the dining room, delicious meals prepared and cooked by Elsie, and had tea in the sitting room. I don't expect any of us appreciated fully at the time the luxury of my grandmother's home. The grand rooms we stayed in, the luxury of having our cases unpacked and our clothes looked after by Mrs Spencer, the housekeeper and wife of Mr Spencer, the butler, who served our meals. On Elsie's day off my grandmother would take everyone staying to dinner at the Lygon Arms.

* *

Another interesting insight into what family life was like at Dumbleton Hall was described in J. M. Scott's marvellous biography of Gino Watkins (The details of this are given in Chapter Seven to accompany his memorial in the church). J. M. Scott in his acknowledgments to his book wrote very movingly about an amazing friend and fellow human being:

'To write the life story of the best friend a man could know is fundamentally a selfish business. To me it gave the right to live again the part I shared with him and, flourishing the search warrant of a biographer, to peer greedily into the memories of others.

....Therefore if there is any merit in this book, it belongs to those friends of Gino Watkins. They are each a part of the story as they were a part of his life. Among them I can only mention his father, who did so much to help me before he died, and Gino's sister, my wife, who told me those things that few remember and that none record, but which are the essence of a character.'

H. G. Watkins

Stanley Baldwin the then Prime Minster wrote of Gino:

'Gino Watkins was a man, a boy, I was going to say, whom I had the pleasure of knowing. If he had lived, he might have ranked, and in the opinion of men qualified to judge, would have ranked, among the greatest of Polar explorers.

They talk about decadence in this country!'

The descriptions in the book involving Dumbleton are really moving and today one can imagine Gino and his family enjoying the home of Lord and Lady Monsell as a happy home:

'*At Dumbleton there were ponies to ride, a lake with boats, and cousins of their own age. Gino went to a day school in London, but for nearly a year, while he was considered too delicate to go to boarding school he shared a governess with his cousin Diana Eyres-Monsell at Dumbleton.*

Smoothly and happily he passed his first seven years.

One day in August 1914 Gino was sitting on the lawn at Dumbleton watching his father and uncle playing tennis. He saw a footman come out of the house with a telegram. The game stopped. The peaceful world he had known was changed in an instant. The house-party dispersed within two hours; and a fortnight later his father was in France with his regiment, the Coldstream Guards.

After his father went to fight, Gino used to say goodnight to his father's photograph, and pray earnestly for his return.

At Dumbleton he had written his first letter. 'My dear Father. How goes it. How many German soldiers have you killed lately. We are having a lovely time here and I can very nearly read. We play at scouting often. I am making a scarf for you and I am making it all myself. I should love to join in the fighting. We go fishing on the lake. I hope you are having a very nice time. Love and kisses from Gino.'

Later after being at public school, the family remained close. Lilliput had been sold and in 1925 they moved from Eaton Place to Onslow Crescent but London and Dumbleton were still their chief haunts. J. M. Scott gives a moving description of what Dumbleton was like at Christmas:

'*But Dumbleton was an ideal place for Christmas, with its big rooms, decorated with holly and mistletoe, great blazing logs in open fireplaces and wonderful meals for which a score of children and their parents sat down together at one table. No doubt their nannies were discussing them upstairs. There was the Christmas breakfast with presents piled on each plate, the dance, the village Christmas tree, the church and the carols and the visits to the well-scrubbed dairy with the prize cards on the wall, where the more cream the children drank the widely Nurden smiled.*

The Dumbleton Dixies gave a performance in the village hall. The cousins blackened their faces, danced, and played what instruments they could find; and Gino with Smith, the jovial chauffeur sang a duet of 'I'm Alabamy Bound' till Smith's enthusiasm broke all the strings of his ukulele.......

Out of doors there was wild boating on the lake and bronco-busting on the bad tempered little donkey. There was hunting and pheasant shooting, the birds streaming past high off

Oxhill, and Gino shouting excitedly, 'Daddy, you must get the next one, Uncle Bobby has had three running.' Mrs Watkins was delighted to see the children so happy with their cousins. Gino adored her and thought her more beautiful than anybody in the world. They had good times together at Dumbleton.

Gino with his sister; with his cousin, Diana Eyres-Monsell; and with his Mother:-courtesy of J. M. Scott 'Gino Watkins' and permission of Susan Casey the granddaughter of Lord and Lady Monsell and daughter of Diana(c).

After Cambridge Gino looked to the future and his choice and fascination was polar exploration. He enjoyed coming back to Dumbleton when he could:

'He spent Christmas and New Year's Day with his family at Dumbleton, here. He took his sister to her first hunt ball, trying to overcome her nervousness by telling her how marvellous she looked in her new dress. He came back to London to spend his days working at the Royal Geographical Society, and his evenings, to the delight of his mother, in parties at home or going out to the theatres and dances with his sister and his friends.'

Gino disappeared on 20th August 1932, aged just 25 out kayaking while polar exploring – a tragedy indeed. J. M. Scott's words on the event were truly poignant:

'They searched till midnight when the northern lights appeared, wavering mysterious and beautiful above the hills which pointed to the stars. They searched all the next day.

But Gino Watkins had gone from this world in the full pride of his youth and self-sufficiency; gone cleanly out leaving no relic of mortality; leaving only the memory of a vivid life and a bright inspiration.

He was always appropriate, and it was right that none should see him dead.'

* *

Lord Monsell enjoyed his work as Chief Whip and was closely consulted by Stanley Baldwin on specific appointments and parliamentary strategy.

OMMANDER EYRES-MONSEL'

Bolton Meredith Eyres-Monsell, 1st Viscount Monsell by Tom Cottrell 1929:- Courtesy of the NPG©

He was **knighted on the 28th June 1929** and acted as *Chief Whip* during the first emergency National Government and then joined the cabinet as **First Lord of the Admiralty** on 5ᵗʰ November 1931.

Sir Bolton Eyres- Monsell as First Lord of the Admiralty

The Eyres-Monsells besides living at *Admiralty House* which was the official residence of the First Lord of the Admiralty, also had a house at one time in Eaton Square and also at *19 Belgrave Square. Cyril Richardson* was a 15 year old '*Hall Boy*' who was one of the servants who came down from Dumbleton to look after the family when they were staying in London.

Cyril has sent me a letter which contains his memories of being the 'Hall Boy' for the Monsell family. Cyril was born at Dumbleton on the 3ʳᵈ September 1921 and his 18ᵗʰ birthday was by chance the same date that Britain declared war on Germany for the Second World War. His grandfather was George Pulley, the village blacksmith, who worked with the 'Straight' family (see Susan Oldacre '*The Blacksmith's Daughter*) and his aunt Connie Pulley ran the Estate poultry farm which supplied the Hall and the Eyres-Monsell London residence. Cyril in his letter gives us an interesting insight into his time at Dumbleton and in London with the family:

26ᵗʰ January 2015

....I have given some thought to what I can remember from my time as the Hall Boy – and the most junior member of the household at Dumbleton Hall – which was from cApril 1937 until c May 1938. Of those 13 months, I think about at least five were spent in two spells at 19 Belgrave Square which had been the London residence from the time of Mrs Eyres, of whom my mother used to speak, having herself been a member of staff. The

184

year 1937 being the coronation year of George VII, I recall being warned to be packed and ready to board the Hall bus with the remainder of the travelling staff en- oute to Evesham GWR and then to Paddington and on to Belgravia by taxi cabs, this taking place soon after joining- it was all go!

19 Belgrave Square in 2015:- JRH©

I was interested to read your description of the Hall Boy's duties in 1901 and can say that by 1937 they had become a bit different, for example I never cleaned footwear. I think the 'Odd Job Man' of whom there was one at the Hall and one at 19 Belgrave Square, would have done these sorts of chores.

At both locations there were staff dining and recreation rooms; these were the Housekeepers Room and the Servants Hall, where the dining tables were headed by the butler and the first footman, respectively. I had to lay the tables for meals for both rooms and clear everything away afterwards to the kitchen. All such meals were taken about one hour before the meal times of the family which was the real activity of each day.

My main workplace was the butler's pantry and involved collecting trays from the servery containing the residue of each course as removed from the dining room by the footmen. I would retain the silver and glass in the pantry and take the remainder to the kitchen and return to the pantry and begin washing up the silver and glass. Before the silver was used again it would be cleaned by the footmen for which purpose the large table was covered with green baize. My other jobs were to answer the tradesmen's door and to keep the floor of the long hallway clean. I would also be required to take letters to post and when at the

Hall, I would take the opportunity to call and see my grandparents. When at No. 19 I would often meet another Hall Boy on similar duties and we became friends. I sometimes was given instructions to collect goods from Harrods in Knightsbridge which as I remember was opposite a Martin's Bank which had connections with the Holland-Martin family and connections with Dumbleton.

As a young member of staff I also remember being given instructions to find my way to Mount Street off Park Lane to the tailors the family used, so that I could have my suit measured.

Yes, I lived in as did all the household staff, except the Butler and the Odd-Job man. The male staff accommodation was separated at the Hall by separate staircases which included individual bedrooms. It was much more cramped at Belgrave Square of course, where the staff ate, worked and slept in the basement. I got on well with all the other members of staff, especially the first footman (who later became a valet for Lord Beaverbrook) and the cook, who in later years married an Uncle of mine and featured in the BBC interview we spoke about.

19 Belgrave Square, sited next door to the Austrian Embassy. The square is one of the largest and grandest 19th century squares in London. It is the centerpiece of Belgravia and was laid out by the property contractor Thomas Cubitt for the 2nd Earl of Gloucester, later the 1st Marquis of Westminster.

My maternal grandparents being long term residents in Dumbleton, where my grandfather was a blacksmith, I knew the village and many of the villagers too. Lady Monsell was a benefactor of course and I believe hers was the drive behind the shop known as the Co-op which had a branch in North Street, Winchcombe. I think I spoke to her ladyship on only *one or two occasions and never to Lord Monsell. I seem to think the marriage was dissolved in due course.*

With just one half day off per week, I had found life too restricted and when my Dad was moved from Winchcombe to Cheltenham Post Office and the family home was there too, I decided to join them and leave the Hall. I soon started with working with Gloster Aircraft at Brockworth which, after WW2 service in the Royal Air Force, proved to be the first step in my long career in the Aircraft cum Aerospace industry.

Yours sincerely

Cyril G. Richardson

The Rt Hon. Sir Bolton Eyres-Monsell MP., GBE. & Lady Eyres-Monsell CBE

He was the longest serving First Sea Lord of the 1930s and he began to restore confidence in the Navy after the shock of the *'Invergordon Mutiny'* and the uncertainty of Field's period as First Sea Lord. In 1932 Monsell decided to replace Field with the outstanding figure of the day, *Admiral Sir Ernle Chatfield*, with whom he established a good working relationship based on their mutual respect for one another and their roles in government. Under the economic pressure of the early 1930s, Monsell *'had to struggle on behalf of the Navy against his old friends in the Cabinet, which was a severe trial to his nature.'* The government were still entrenched in the *'Appeasement'* policy and had no wish to start expanding the Army, Air Force or the Navy. In Chatfield's view *'no one could have done more, few could have achieved so much' (Lord Chatfield, 'It Might Happen Again' II,p.98).*

In April 1936 an article appeared in British Newspapers and in the '*New York Times*', which today appears to us incredulous, that a German Ambassador could be accorded such honours, but in retrospect the public and politicians at the time had no idea of what would take place so soon after this event.

'HOESCH IS HONORED IN BRITISH CORTEGE; Eden in Procession with the Swastika-Draped Coffin of the German Ambassador. 19-GUN SALUTE BOOMS OUT Bingham Among Diplomats in State March in London -- Body Is Borne Away on Warship.

LONDON, April 15. -- Wrapped in a Nazi swastika flag, the body of Dr. Leopold von Hoesch, German Ambassador to Great Britain, left Dover aboard a British destroyer today on its way to the family vault at Dresden.

The Daily Sketch on the 15th April 1936 also mentioned this event in the following article:

FAREWELL TO AMBASSADOR -- Herr Von Hoesch's Last Journey Home

'*The Daily Sketch*' gave a list of those who were present in full ceremonial dress for the funeral and these included:

Lord Monsell, First Lord of the Admiralty, *Sir John Simon, Home Secretary, Mr. Anthony Eden, Foreign Secretary, Baron de Marchienne the Belgium Ambassador, Mr. R. W. Bingham the United States Ambassador, Signor Grandi the Italian Ambassador and M. Corbin, the French Ambassador.*

The body of Herr von Hoesch, German Ambassador to London who died suddenly last Friday, was conveyed from his home in Carlton House Terrace to Victoria past great crowds of silent spectators. The coffin, which rested on a gun carriage, was draped with the red and white Nazi flag.

Below are British representatives and diplomats of other countries walking in the funeral procession.'

The body was taken to Dover where the British destroyer 'Scout' steamed away with the coffin on a gun platform in the stern guarded by naval ratings for the journey to Wilhelmshaven. The gun platform between the funnels was a mass of wonderful wreaths.

* *

188

Leopold von Hoesch (10 June 1881 – 10 April 1936) was a career German diplomat. He had started his career as the *charge d' affaires* in France in 1923 after the 'Ruhr Crisis'. He moved on to become the head of the German Embassy in Paris.

Leopold von Hoesch (on left), 1932

In 1932 Hoesch was transferred to the United Kingdom as the German Ambassador, a post he retained until his sudden and suspicious death in 1936. He was generally well liked in England and his reputation as a knowledgeable and able-minded statesman helped to support the Anglo-German relationship during the early 1930s.

When the Nazis took over in 1933, at first there were few changes in the relationship between the United Kingdom and the new Germany, but by 1934 Hoesch began to challenge Hitler indirectly and in due course their relationship became more difficult. Hoesch died suddenly of a heart attack while dressing in his bedroom at the German Embassy on 11th April 1936, which appeared rather suspicious in the circumstances and useful for Hitler who was finding his Ambassador becoming *'a thorn in his side'.*

The state funeral of Leopold von Hoesch. His coffin was hoisted onto a gun carriage at Carlton Place. The spectators giving the Nazi salute within sight of Buckingham Palace is in itself extraordinary!

He was given a full military funeral and his coffin transported back to Germany on board a British warship, '*HMS Scout.*'

HMS Scout-one of 12 naval ships carrying this name

His replacement was the notorious *Joachim von Ribbentrop*, Hitler's favorite foreign policy advisor, later to be hanged in 1946 for war crimes.

The Anglo-German Naval Agreement of 1935 was the most controversial event of Monsell's career. Although he signed it on Britain's behalf, it originated as a German offer

191

and was shaped by many hands. Winston Churchill attacked the agreement at the time and in his later memoirs, and for many years after the Second World War, it was regarded as a defining example of the folly of appeasement. It has been said that the **First Lord of the Admiralty**, invited Von Ribbentrop to **Dumbleton** for talks on the agreement in 1936 , although the talks would have been in secret so no photographs or evidence that he was at Dumbleton exists. It was said Ribbentrop left silk curtain material for the Hall with the swastika embroidered on them. I doubt they would have been hung up and probably quickly either disposed of or hidden away in case of a return visit! I have a quote given me by Mr Martin Grafton the Archivist of a note given to him by an Ivy Finlayson who had connections with the Hall:

'Ribbentrop gave the curtains – possibly dark blue – they hung at the windows opposite the lift – the snooker room is where the 'Shire' room is now. Ivy believes it was Ribbentrop who had earmarked Dumbleton to take over, not Hitler after Germany had conquered England.'

Mr Martin Grafton, the Dumbleton Hall archivist, in his research received a letter from *Patrick Leigh Fermor* sent from *'The Mill House'* in Dumbleton in response to the question of whether Ribbentrop had ever been to Dumbleton and his reply is interesting:

'Ribbentrop did stay at Dumbleton during the 1930s. Of course the Anglo-German Pact was going on then...'

It was probably Ribbentrop who gave Lord Monsell the invitation for the 1936 Olympic Games in Berlin- but no record of him attending this event can be found although on the back of the invitation, Monsell had written the word *'Accepted'* which looks as if he did go. He certainly was in Germany with *Lord Halifax* a short time later.

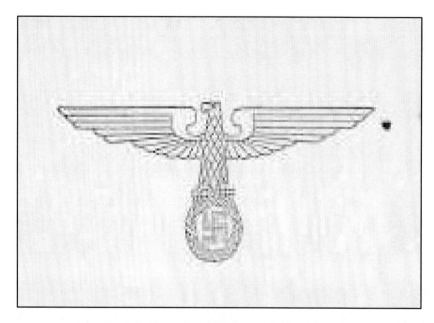

IM NAMEN DER REICHSREGIERUNG
BITTEN DIE REICHSMINISTER
GENERALOBERST GÖRING UND DR. GOEBBELS
AUS ANLASS DER
XI. OLYMPISCHEN SPIELE BERLIN 1936
_____ Lord   Monsell / _____
ZU EINEM EMPFANG IN DER STAATSOPER BERLIN
AM 6. AUGUST 1936 · ABENDS 20ᵘ UHR

The invitation to Lord Monsell to the 1936 Olympic Games in Berlin

* *

Ulrich Friedrich Wilhelm Joachim von Ribbentrop -1893-1946 – was the Foreign Minister of Nazi Germany from 1938 until 1945. He was appointed the German Ambassador to Britain in 1936 after the sudden and somewhat suspicious death of the popular former ambassador *Leopold Von Hoesch.*

Ribbentrop first came to the attention of Adolf Hitler as a well travelled businessman with more knowledge and experience of the world outside Germany than most of the other Nazi officials who served in the party.

He came to Hitler's attention when he offered his house for the secret talks in January 1933 which resulted in Hitler being appointed the Chancellor of Germany, the second highest position in Germany after the President, which Hindenburg still held.

He became a close confidant of the *Führer,* but this was unpopular with the other party members who considered Ribbentrop to be lacking in talent, superficial and a sycophant. He was however appointed *Ambassador to Britain* in 1936 and then *Germany's Foreign Minister* in February 1938.

Just before the start of the Second World War he played a key role in the brokering of the *'Pact of Steel'* (with fascist Italy and Mussolini) and also the Soviet-German non-aggression pact with Stalin, known as the *'Molotov-Ribbentrop Pact'.* After 1941 his influence in key decisions in Nazi Germany declined.

In 1945 he was tried for war crimes at *Nuremberg,* a city he knew well from the many spectacular Nazi Rallies of Hitler. He was convicted of war crimes and also knowing and allowing the *'Holocaust'* to happen. On 16th October 1946 he became the first of those sentenced to death, due to *Hermann Goring's* suicide moments before he would have been sentenced to death.

Ribbentrop's two years as the German Ambassador in London – 1936-38 was not considered a success after the popularity of the former ambassador. Within hours of arriving in London he had used the platform at Victoria station to flout protocol by calling on Britain to join Germany on a crusade against the *'Bolshevik menace'.* An even greater gaff was that it was reported that he gave the *'Heil Hitler'* salute to George VI when presenting his credentials at Buckingham Palace. The German Embassy was also guarded by the 'SS' and his massive Mercedes flew the Nazi flag. He was not popular with the public and officialdom became frustrated with the enormous amount of time he spent out of the country. He was still head of the *'Ribbentrop Organization'* which was an instrument of foreign policy, which was often at odds with our own foreign policy. This organization was financed by the party – he had been given the rank and uniform of a colonel in the 'SS' and was responsible only to Hitler.

Ribbentrop was thought by Hitler to be the ideal candidate for the position of Ambassador to London as he spoke perfect English having spent three years living in Canada before the war. He had successfully carried through the *'Anglo-German Naval Agreement'* the year before and had influential friends, but his arrogance, driving ambition, his bad manners and his worship of Hitler and the Nazi regime did not endear him to London.

Adolf Hitler himself had lost faith in his disciple's role as the ambassador, and even referred to him as a *'champagne salesman'*. This of course had been a perfectly sensible career for an unemployed ex-serviceman, but also caused much jealousy on his success and in marrying *Annalies Henkell* of the Champagne family. Unfortunately he allied himself with the Nazis as part of his ambition for greatness. His devotion to Hitler was unquestionable and even at the end while in Nuremberg awaiting trial he had been asked by the prison psychiatrist if he had ever contemplated assassinating his master, to which he had replied it would have been like *'killing my own father.'* Ribbentrop was said on reflection to be stubborn, truculent and humourless, and a typical Nazi.

Ribbentrop was hanged because he allowed his ministry to be active participants in the deportation and atrocities which were committed in Russia and Poland as well as the other occupied countries. He did meet his death with dignity and courage, which was one of his few virtues.

* *

Monsell had decided to retire from politics in 1935, but was persuaded to remain due to the approaching international naval disarmament conference in London. Monsell had also been persuaded to be its chairman. He did retire from the House of Commons at the time of the 1935 general election, and was raised to the peerage as **Viscount Monsell** on the 30th November 1935. He eventually stood down as First Lord on 5th June 1936, by which time the negotiations for the **London Naval Treaty** had been concluded. The conference failed to secure any significant disarmament, in the threat of Hitler's continuing rise to power, but again there did not take place an unbridled arms race.

Viscount Eyres-Monsell: - courtesy of the NPG London©

The **Anglo-German Naval Agreement** took place in the June of 1935 and allowed Hitler to build new ships up to 35 per cent of the strength of the Royal Navy and this would include battleships, cruisers, aircraft carriers and later submarines.

These concessions were regarded as poor and allowed Hitler to become even more reckless. This at the time also offended Britain's closest ally, France. The agreement went against Britain's international undertakings and grossly breached the terms of the 'Treaty of Versailles.' Lord Monsell, the then first lord of the Admiralty said: 'the naval staff were satisfied and had been anxious to bring about an agreement'. Stabilization of Anglo-German naval competition would release Royal Navy ships to sail to distant waters-perhaps many at the conference believed that by showing goodwill towards the Nazis would bring lasting peace; it may have also been thought that a more powerful Fascist Germany would keep Communist Russia contained.

Significantly, perhaps, Hitler immediately renamed the *Reichmarine* the *Kriegsmarine* and German began building ships immediately. Germany's largest battleships, the

'*Scharnhorst, Gneisenau, Bismarck,* and *Tirpitz,* which would later give the British navy so much trouble, were laid down as an immediate result of this treaty. The following year Germany agreed – in the *London Submarine Protocol* of 3ʳᵈ September 1936 – that it would adhere strictly to the international prize law, which provided for the safety of merchant ship passengers and crew in time of war.

The German battleship 'Bismarck'

From 1941 to 1945 Monsell served as **Regional Controller of Civil Defence** for the south-east of England. He had one son and three daughters, but was said to have been rather a remote figure to his children, who rarely saw very much of their father when they were growing up. By the 1940s his first marriage was effectively over, and he did not defend his wife's suit for divorce on the grounds of adultery. The decree for the ending of the marriage was granted on the 25ᵗʰ May 1950, and exactly two months later Monsell remarried. His second wife, *Essex Leila Hilary French (1907-1996),* was the grand-daughter of the first *Earl of Ypres* and had been previously married to *Captain Vyvyan Drury.* Monsell died on the 21ˢᵗ March 1969 following an aneurism in his leg; he was cremated on the 28ᵗʰ March and his ashes scattered at sea from a naval warship.

* *

An interesting article appeared in the *Gloucester Echo* with connections with **Dumbleton** at the end of the War. It is dated 31ˢᵗ December 1946:

'For 45 years the head gardener at Dumbleton Hall & prominent church worker, Mr Lambert Gillett, who retained all his activity and interest in his work up to the time he was admitted to Winchcombe Hospital about 2 weeks ago, has died at the age of 82.

Mr Gillett who is survived by his wife (his daughter died after an operation some six months ago) was a native of Bourton on the Water. In his younger days he was employed at Brockhampton Park. For the past 45 years he supervised the Dumbleton Hall Gardens. A noted horticulturalist he served as a judge and was very much sought after by organisers of local shows and he was in this capacity a frequent visitor to Cheltenham and Evesham.'

During the war, the Hall gardens were partly devoted to commercial food production. He supervised their management for Viscount and Viscountess Monsell.'

During the War Dumbleton Hall was used by the *'Woman's Land Army'*

The late *Joan Betteridge* of Badsey had written an excellent first hand description of what it was like to be billeted in such a fine house as Dumbleton- (This article was first published on Thursday 5ᵗʰ April 2001)

'In 1943, Dumbleton Hall was opened as a Womans Land Army hostel and continued until the early 1950s.

I was in the WLA at Mickleton in 1942 and in July 1943, I was sent to Dumbleton Hall with about 20 girls to start this hostel there. Girls also came from Shurdington and various other places.

We did not want to leave Mickleton. We were in a lovely house there. We were taken by lorry to Dumbleton. I will never forget the journey. We went through the hall gates and up the long drive and we really thought we had come to a palace.

Some photographs showing the sort of work the land girls were expected to do.

It really is the most beautiful house and we had the entire top floor for bedrooms and bathrooms, kitchens and dining room and a huge lounge (wc room) downstairs.

We loved it all, the house and the lovely grounds. We were taken by lorry every day to work on the farms and although it was land work I just loved it.

It is especially precious to me as I met my husband at the dance at the Dumbleton village Hall. We did all our courting (eight months) in the gardens of the hall.

Dumbleton Hall has many happy memories for us ex-land girls. I keep in contact with about a dozen girls and we do meet up often and when we do it's all talk of Dumbleton Hall.

I did just want to let you know of those years that the Hall belonged to the Land Army. Lady Monsell was there when we were and she was very interested in our work. I left to be married in 1945 but have been back a few times and really love it.

A Post Office Stamp Issued to show a typical Land Girl, coincidentally, the Post Office would later buy Dumbleton Hall

Mr Martin Purches wrote to me about his Mother who was a Land Girl at Dumbleton. Her name was Muriel Dicks and at 87 still has some marvellous memories of her time at Dumbleton Hall:

Muriel Purches (nee Dicks)

Muriel Dicks was born on the 28ʰ May 1928. Her parents, Ethel and Donald Dicks lived in Filton, Bristol.

Muriel was the second of four children. Her older sister Joan had suffered TB as a child and was 'delicate and sickly'. As 'Mum's pet' she was also mostly exempt from the household chores. Muriel was therefore responsible for the care of her two younger siblings, Doreen and Brian. Muriel well remembers WW2. The family home was close to the British Aircraft Company factories which were frequently targeted by the Luftwaffe.

Muriel remembers seeing low flying bombers over Filton and recalls great excitement amongst the young children, they being unaware of the danger.

In April 1945, after hearing that she had been accepted by the WLA and aged just 17, she set off to take up her posting at Dumbleton Hall in the Cotswolds.

Dumbleton Hall in 1945:- courtesy of Mrs Muriel Purches and her son Martin©

Upon her arrival at Dumbleton, Muriel was staggered by the grandeur of the house and parkland. She recalls a welcome briefing by an older supervisor before being shown to her bedroom on the top floor of the Hall. She shared her room with two other girls (one named Linda). There were between 20 and 25 Land Girls billeted at the Hall most of the time during her stay. Friendships were made, but some of the groups were rather 'cliquey' thinking themselves a cut above the others.

Life at Dumbleton was exciting. Muriel met girls from all over the country. One in particular, Joan from Manchester, would become a lifelong friend. Joan married a local farm worker named Ted Pulley and the couple lived in a cottage as part of a Dumbleton farmyard for many years after the war. They kept in touch until Joan's death in Moreton-in-Marsh in c2009.

Muriel and a friend at Dumbleton:-courtesy of Mrs Muriel Purches and her son Martin©

Muriel still treasures her photographs taken at Dumbleton and the memories they invoke of 'The Gang' of Land Girls. The gang included Margaret Lewis (married to Stan), Jean (married to George) Humphries, Netta, Jean Curtis, Olly Kemp and 'Ray'.

Muriel also enjoyed meeting and chatting to the locals, all of whom seemed quite colourful to a girl from the city. She remembers in particular an older farm worker known as 'Moby' – a 'lovely man.'

A very pretty Muriel Dicks with one of the Estate workers 'a lovely old man just called Moby':-
courtesy of Muriel Purches and her son Martin©

On workdays the girls would assemble outside the hall to hear their duties for the day. This might include working in the fields, driving tractors and managing the horses to plough and to tend to the crops. The girls spent most of their time working on the farms attached to the Dumbleton estate but were also on occasions loaned out to other farmers further away. The girls looked forward to the variety offered by these 'away days' and would happily climb aboard farm lorries and trailers to be taken off to their place of work-

singing the popular songs of the day as they went. They often came back loaded with fruit and vegetables – gifts from grateful farmers. With food rationing still in place this was a fantastic supplement to their diet. When possible the girls would take these supplies home to help their families.

Work was often hard and dusty, but on return to the Hall at the end of the day, the girls had the luxury of a bath. A bath every day – 'Mum would have gone berserk!'

Meals at Dumbleton Hall were served from the large kitchens on the ground floor. The girls would line up along the corridors and collect their meal from a hatch. Food tended to be simple – bread, margarine and jam were staples - but at least there was plenty of it.

Muriel recalls that her wages had been £1.50 per week. She had to pay rent and 'keep' from this and felt obliged to send £1.00 of it back to Mum. The rest was hers to spend!

Muriel with Mary Folkestone- 1948

Muriel has a few memories of the owners of Dumbleton, though recalls being told on some occasions to avoid certain parts of the house and grounds when Lord and Lady Monsell were in residence. Muriel believes they may have spent some time at nearby Alderton – perhaps to avoid their rather wild and noisy guests! She does recalls experiencing a taste of a grand and very different lifestyle – involving butlers, staff and expensive cars.

Off-duty hours were spent in common rooms at Dumbleton, chatting, playing games and listening to the radio. Some of the girls had brought records which they played on a radiogram.

Occasionally there would be a dance night at Dumbleton Hall. On other occasions the girls would have a night out at a local pub or perhaps a dance at a local village hall. On such occasions the girls would troop down the drive to the main Evesham road where they would cheerfully hitch a lift. Muriel recalls some fun nights out at nearby Alderton. They would often walk to Alderton across the hills.

Mum, Margaret and Netta in 1946: courtesy of Martin Purches and his Mother Muriel©

Muriel stayed at Dumbleton until 1947, returning to the family home and an office job at BAC where she later met her husband Bertie, but she never forgot Dumbleton and had a lifelong love of the Cotswolds. She returned to Dumbleton in 2015 for a family reunion at the hotel and was able to talk to her great grandchildren about the great times she had here as a teenager.

Jean Curtis at 'the walk' – Dumbleton 1948

Betty and Olly in 1949

Jean and George in 1947

Christmas card from Dumbleton:-courtesy of Muriel and her son Martin Purches©

The Gang in 1947

Eileen, Joan, Netta, Margaret & Muriel in 1946

Land Girls Parade in Bristol (entering the Centre from Park Street) - 1946

'Brumie' & 'Spud' Murphy

Muriel, Rusty & Ron 1948

Muriel with fiancé Bertie in 1950

Muriel in 1949

'Olly' at Hinton's, Alderton- 1949

* *

Lord Monsell's second daughter, the Hon Joan Eyres-Monsell (1912-2003), was married for the second time in 1968 to Patrick Leigh Fermor, the great traveller and author. His story and connection with the family and with Dumbleton will be looked at in the next chapter.

The Hon Joan Eyres-Monsell and Patrick Leigh Fermor

A suburb of Leicester is named 'Eyres Monsell' after the family; the council estate was built on land they had owned before it was compulsorily purchased in the early 1950s.

Lord Bolton Eyres-Monsell had a private funeral service and his ashes were scattered at sea on 27th May 1969 from *HMS Wakeful* by the Rev. N.M. Denlegh-Maxwell RN.

There is a memorial window dedicated to Lord Eyres-Monsell in *St Olave's* Hart Street, London.

St Olave Hart Street - is a Church of England church in the City of London, situated on the corner of Hart Street and Seething Lane near the Fenchurch Street station.

John Betjeman described St Olave's as 'a country church in the world of Seething Lane, perhaps this is why Lord Monsell liked to worship here, as it may have reminded him of Dumbleton. The church is one of the smallest in the City and is one of only a handful of medieval churches which survived the 'Great Fire of London' in 1666. As well as being the local parish church, St Olave's is the Ward Church of the Tower Ward of the City of London.

The church is first recorded in the 13ᵗʰ century as '*St Olav-towards-the-Tower.*' A stone building replaced the earlier (presumably wooden) construction. It is dedicated to the patron saint of Norway, King Olaf II of Norway who fought alongside the Anglo-Saxon King Ethelred the Unready against the Danes in the Battle of London Bridge in 1014. He was canonized after his death and the church of St Olave was apparently built on the site of the battleground. The Norwegian connection was reinforced during the Second World War when Haakon VII of Norway worshipped there while in exile.

St Olave's Church, Hart Street in London

Mr Manning sent me the following information on the above window:

The Monsell Memorial Window – *was designed and executed by John Hayward and occupies the three small lights above the South Porch. It was dedicated in a short, simple service attended by Lady Monsell and other members of the family, the Deputy Master and other representatives of Trinity House.*

Trinity House has an annual service here at Trinity tide which is attended by the Master, the Court and Younger Brethren, as well as staff and pensioners. Trinity House has a window in the south-east corner of the church, installed as part of the post-war restoration of the church in the 1950s and we also have a model of a lightship in a glass case.

* *

Chapter Six: Stories and Legends Associated with Dumbleton Hall and the Village

The name 'Dumbleton' has a pleasurable ring to it which has appealed to writers over the years. In 'The Importance of Being Earnest' by Oscar Wilde, Lady Bracknell refers to a '*Lady Dumbleton*,' and in Dorothy L. Sayers in '*Murder Must Advertise*' the village becomes the site of a minor public school.

One of the interesting connections with Dumbleton Hall is a British Collett-built GWR 4900 Class (Hall Class) 4-6-0 steam locomotive, built in Swindon in March 1929. Its first shed allocation was at Old Oak Common. In August 1950 the shed allocation was Reading, and in March 1959 it was allocated to Newton Abbot. The locomotive's last shed allocation was Bristol Barrow Rd. *Dumbleton Hall* was withdrawn from British Railways service in December 1965 and sold to Woodham Brothers scrapyard in Barry, South Wales.

It was sold to BTSR, Buckfastleigh and left as the 82nd departure from Barry in June 1976 before being fully restored in 1988. It is currently stored out of use at Buckfastleigh on the South Devon Railway, awaiting overhaul. The engine is in its Great Western Railway green livery.

The 4900 Class locomotive 'Dumbleton Hall':- courtesy of the South Devon Railway Society©

Dumbleton Hall, as might be expected, has its ghost. A grey lady has been seen in recent times mounting the stairs. But the real village ghost seems to be a white lady who walks round the fish pond by the cricket field at midnight and then across what is now Garden Close.

A poltergeist is occasionally experienced in the lounge and bar which flings the drinks across the table. It is a little worrying when guests are around!

It has been noted by a senior long-standing member of staff that the handle on the door from the reception area into the library will start to turn before he gets close to it, as if there is someone on the other side opening the door- all very strange!

* *

One of the most interesting characters in more recent years associated with Dumbleton is *Sir Patrick Leigh Fermor*, whose recent publication *'Abducting a General'* published by John Murray in 2014 has brought this amazing personality back into the public eye. He is a worthy celebrity to be associated with the history of Dumbleton and the Hall. Patrick was married to Lord and Lady Eyres-Monsell's daughter Joan.

Sir Patrick Michael Leigh Fermor, DSO, OBE – 11th February 1915- 10th June 2011 was a British author, scholar, and soldier who is best remembered for his prominent role behind the scenes in the Cretan resistance during the Second World War. He was also well known and often cited during his lifetime as being *'Britain's greatest living travel writer.'* One BBC journalist once described him as being a cross between Indiana Jones, James Bond and Graham Greene.

Patrick Michael Leigh Fermor by Mark Gerson in February 1954:- courtesy of the NPG©

He was born in London the son of Sir Lewis Leigh Fermor a distinguished geologist and Muriel Aeyleen, daughter of Charles Taafe Ambler. Shortly after his birth his parents and his sister left him in England while they travelled to India, and it would be another four years before they met again.

Patrick attended the *King's School* in Canterbury but had problems with his schoolwork, He was later expelled from the school having being seen holding the hand of the greengrocer's daughter!

In his last report from the school he was described as *'a dangerous mixture of sophistication and recklessness.'* After his expulsion, he home taught himself by reading texts on Greek, Latin, and Shakespeare and he also enjoyed history. He had wanted to join the Royal Military College at Sandhurst, but later changed his mind and concentrated on being a writer.

In 1933 he left his friends in London to travel in Europe. At 18 years of age he decided to walk the length of Europe, from the Hook of Holland to Constantinople. He set off on the 8th December, the year after Hitler had come to power, but was not yet Chancellor in Germany. He spent time on his travels in barns, shepherds' huts, and monasteries but was also invited by many of the landed gentry to stay at their country houses in Europe. Two of his later travel books *'A Time of Gifts'* (1977) and *'Between the Woods and the Water'* (1968), were based on this journey. A book on the final part of this journey was unfinished at the time of Leigh Fermor's death, but published in 2013 by John Murray. This was based on Leigh Fermor's diary at the time and on an earlier draft from the 1960s.

He arrived at the end of his epic European journey on the 1st January 1935, and then decided to continue his travels to Greece. In March he became involved in the campaign of royalist forces in Macedonia against the attempted Republican revolt. In Athens he met *Balasha Cantacuzene*, a Romanian Phanariote noblewoman, with whom he fell in love.

Balasha Cantacuzene

They shared an old watermill outside the city where he wrote and she painted. They moved to Baleni, Galati, and the Cantacuzene house in Moldavia, where they were living at the outbreak of the Second World War.

Leigh Fermor was an active member of the resistance during the Second World War. As an officer cadet he had trained alongside Iain Moncreiffe and Derek Bond and later had joined the Irish Guards. He was proficient in Greek and later was commissioned to become a liaison officer in the General list in August 1940 in Albania. He fought in Crete and also on the mainland of Greece after the German occupation and returned to Crete three times, once by parachute.

In the *Special Operations Executive* (SOE), he disguised himself as *'Michalis or Filemem'* a shepherd and helped to organize the resistance to the German occupation. He lived for over two years in the mountains with Captain Bill Stanley Moss as his second in command.

He is remembered particularly when on 26th April 1944 he captured and evacuated the German commander, *General Heinrich Kreipe.* In his recently reprinted book '*Abducting a General*' he goes into detail how he and his small group accomplished the task. The daring plan was hatched to abduct the general while ensuring that no reprisals were taken against the Cretan population. Dressed as German military police, Patrick and Bill Moss stopped and took control of Kreipe's car, drove through twenty-two German checkpoints, and then succeeded in hiding from the German army before being finally picked up on a beach to the south of the island and transported to safety in Egypt on 14th May.

Members of the Kreipe abduction team: Georgios Tyrakis, William Stanley Moss, Leigh Fermor (dressed in German uniform), Emmanouil Paterakis and Antonios Papaleonidas

General Heinrich Kreipe

General Heinrich Kreipe participated in the Battle of France and was the commander of the 209 of the 58th infantry regiment and took part in *Operation Barbarossa* in the drive towards Leningrad. He was awarded the *Knight's Cross of the Iron Cross* on 13th October 1941. He remained in the Leningrad front until May 1942, when he returned to Germany where he took up administrative and teaching posts.

In June to October 1943 he returned to the Eastern Front, where he led the 79th Infantry Division.

On 1st March 1944, Kreipe operated on Crete as Commander of the 22nd Air Landing Infantry Division. He replaced General Friedrich-Wilhelm Muller.

Patrick Leigh Fermor meeting the General in Athens some years later

There is a memorial commemorating Kreipe's abduction near Archanes in Crete to this day.

Moss featured the events of the abduction in his book '*Ill Met by Moonlight*' which was later adapted as a film (1957) with Leigh Fermor being portrayed by Dirk Bogarde.

Leigh Fermor's wartime Honours included:

Officer of the Most Excellent Order of the British Empire (OBE) and the Distinguished Service Order (DSO), and he was made an Honary Citizen of Heraklion, of Kardamyli and of Gytheio.

The National Archives in London hold copies of his wartime dispatches from occupied Crete in file number HS 5/728 which make for some interesting reading.

Leigh Fermor, photographed by <u>Dimitri Papadimos</u>

After the war, Leigh Fermor published initially his first book '*The Traveller's Tree,*' about his travels in the Caribbean. The book won the '*Heinemann Foundation Prize*' for Literature and established his career as a first class travel writer. He went on to publish other travel books including '*Mani and Roumeli*' about his travels on mule and foot around the remote parts of Greece.

Leigh Fermor was a friend of Lawrence Durrell, who in his book '*Bitter Lemons*' (1957) writes about the Cypriot insurgency against continued British rule in 1955, Leigh Fermor had visited Durrell's villa in Bellapais on Cyprus:

"After a splendid dinner by the fire he starts singing, songs of Crete, Athens, Macedonia. When I go out to refill the <u>ouzo</u> bottle...I find the street completely filled with people listening in utter silence and darkness. Everyone seems struck dumb. 'What is it?' I say, catching sight of Frangos. 'Never have I heard of Englishmen singing Greek songs like this!' Their reverent amazement is touching; it is as if they want to embrace Paddy wherever he goes "

In 1968 after many years together Leigh Fermor married the Honorable Joan Elizabeth Raynor (née Eyres Monsell, the daughter of Bolton Eyres-Monsell, 1ˢᵗ Viscount Monsell. She accompanied him on many of his travels and died in June 2003 at the age of 91.

The couple had no children. They lived part of the year in a house in an olive grove near Kardamyli in the Mani Peninsula in Greece and part of the year in Dumbleton at the 'Mill House'.

Patrick Leigh Fermor was knighted in the 2004 New Year's Honours.

Patrick Fermor's home in Greece at Kalamitsi in September 2014 (see colour plate)

Patrick Leigh Fermor at his home in Dumbleton

The Mill House, Dumbleton, Patrick Leigh Fermor's former home – for sale in 2014 with an asking price of £1,850,000

He was diagnosed as having a cancerous tumour in early 2011 and underwent a tracheotomy in Greece. As his death was becoming closer he expressed a wish to return to England to die. He died there aged 96, on the 10th June 2011, the day after his return.

His funeral took place on the 16th June at St Peter's Church, Dumbleton. A Guard of Honour was provided by serving and former members of the Intelligence Corps, and a bugler from the Irish Guards sounded the Last Post and reveille. He was buried alongside his wife in the churchyard at Dumbleton.

The graves of Patrick Leigh Fermor & his wife Joan Leigh Fermor in St Peter's Churchyard, Dumbleton: - JRH©

An interesting insight into the character of Patrick Leigh Fermor can also be found in the letters he wrote at Dumbleton to *Deborah Devonshire, Duchess of Devonshire*. It all started in the spring of 1956 when, Deborah, Duchess of Devonshire, the youngest of the legendary Mitford sisters invited Patrick to visit *Lismore Castle*, the Devonshire house in Ireland. This well remembered visit sparked off a deep friendship and a lifelong exchange of sporadic and highly entertaining letters. Deborah would have known Dumbleton well having visited with her sisters.

Lismore Castle, Co. Waterford, Ireland

227

The letters from the two friends proved they had much in common, Patrick writing from Dumbleton and the Duchess from the splendour of Chatsworth. In their correspondence they both display their huge enjoyment of life, youthful high spirits, warmth, good humour, generosity and a lack of any malice.

There are glimpses of famous events such as the inauguration of President Kennedy, weekends at Sandringham, stag hunting in France, filming with Errol Flynn in French Equatorial Africa and above all, life at Chatsworth, the great house which the Duchess spent much of her life restoring, and of Paddy in the house he and his wife Joan designed and built on the southernmost peninsula of Greece. These letters are a joy to read and I shall include a couple of extracts which mention in particular Dumbleton.

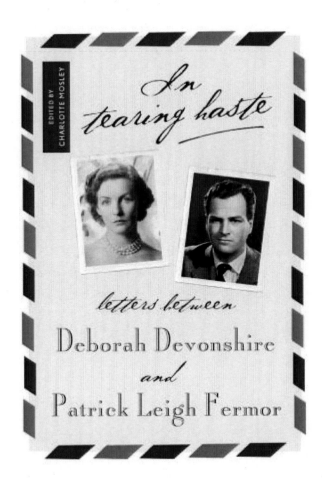

EDITED BY CHARLOTTE MOSLEY

In tearing haste

letters between

Deborah Devonshire

and

Patrick Leigh Fermor

Written from Dumbleton Hall on the 7th July 1957:

....They are mowing the hay here and everything smells marvellous. When this is finished,
I sneak off to the village for a meditative glass of Ind Coope.
Lots of Love
Paddy

A picture during the hay harvest at Dumbleton:-courtesy of the Dumbleton Society and the late Don Caisey©

Sunday (1960)   *Dumbleton, Evesham*

Darling Debo,
I went for aa long walk with Joan & Graham in the Dumbleton woods yesterday, and we found a young fox caught in a trap by one fore-paw. It snarled and glared as we

approached to release him, so I had to pull him by the brush with one hand, opening the trap with the other. Free at last he paused and fixed me with a glance of implacable hatred, then limped off sensibly, into a jungle of foxgloves. If it had been a lion, far from saving my life like Androcles years later in the Coliseum, he would have swallowed me there and then. I minced on my way rather crestfallen.
Lots of love,
Paddy

After the death of Patrick Leigh Fermor's mother-in-law in 1959, Dumbleton Hall was sold to the Post Office Fellowship of Remembrance as a convalescent home for employees and the family moved into the agent's old house.

* *

Chapter Seven: The Church and the Village of Dumbleton.

Dumbleton is a village on the borders of Worcestershire and Gloucestershire; it is roughly 20 miles from the City of Gloucester and 3 miles from the nearest town which is Evesham. The village can trace its foundations into the distant past and is known to have existed in the time of Ethelred I who granted land here to Abington Abbey. It is also mentioned in the Domesday Book.

Early postcard of Dumbleton c1900:-courtesy of the Dumbleton Society & the late Don Caisey©

A similar view of Dumbleton in January 2015:-JRH©

'Dumbleton' comes from the Anglo-Saxon 'ton' which means a settlement so of ancient foundation. It is sited on the edge of Dumbleton Hill in an area of outstanding natural beauty. It is a beautiful village and has its own shop, school, village hall and fine Norman Church with earlier foundations. The village has an ancient road pattern – which can be seen in the early Kip drawing it was considered a 'model' village from the various houses built for the estate workers, some of which were erected by Edward Holland and some by the Eyres family.

One must also mention the various farms and cottages which were all part of the estate, notably Bank Farm, Cullabine Farm & Leyfield and all played a part in the history of the Hall and the village. Although these farms today are not functioning as such, the physical survival of the buildings is a reminder of life in the past.

Today, the estate shooting rights employ a great deal of people and are an important part of the countryside and the local economy.

One of the finest and most historic houses in the village is 'The Old Rectory' built close to the ancient Church.

The Old Rectory and the fine staircase in the main Hall: - courtesy of Mr and Mrs C. Oliver©

The development and the origin of the Old Rectory has been a subject for debate over many years. I have referred to conversations with Mr Oliver, the present owner, concerning part of the Rectory and to Adrian and Cassandra Phillips who carried out extensive and detailed research into the history of this fine ancient building.

The house and home as it stands today was constructed in the 17th Century. It is today divided into two parts with what is called the north and the south wings. The south wing which is the black and white half-timbered house is 16th Century. The two wings have separate owners.

An interesting feature of the house is to be found at the rear of the building where there is a blocked window which has a painted trompe l'oeil of another window from which the Revd Charles Cocks is seen looking out. His likeness was copied from a painting found in Eastnor Castle.

Trompe l'œil (*French for "deceive the eye")* – this is an art technique that uses realistic imagery, which can create an optical illusion, that has the effect of creating an object or a person in this case in three dimensions. Forced perspective is a comparative illusion in architecture.

The Old Rectory before the half-timbering on the southern part was exposed and the brick chimney was built (c1930?):-courtesy of Adrian and Cassandra Phillips©

The Church of St Peter's, Dumbleton

The Church at Dumbleton is dedicated to St Peter, and is Norman in origin, although more than likely was built on the site of an earlier wooden Saxon church. It has 13th century additions. The chancel was rebuilt in 1862 during a Victorian restoration. In 1960 it was designated a Grade 1 listed building.

St Peter's was in possession of Abingdon Abbey from the Conquest until the Dissolution. The 12th century remains include parts of the north and the south walls of the nave, with sections of the Norman corbel table of carved grotesques which are a fine feature.

The North side doorway and the 12th Century grotesques:-JRH

The chancel inside the church was restored in 1872-3 by *Thomas Collins* of Tewkesbury. Further restoration took place in 1904 and 1905 by *Sidney Kitson of Leeds.* It was at this time that the south porch was added, the north-east vestry and the organ chamber, and most of the present furnishings, especially the Pulpit, Pews and Chancel stalls, all carved with excellent panels of various fruits.

An example of one of the bench ends decorated with fruit and flowers

The pulpit and the lectern part of the 1904/5 restoration

On entering the Church one of the first and most poignant memorials the visitor sees is that to *'Gino' Watkins* the Arctic explorer who was the son of the first Lord Monsell's sister. He had spent a lot of time at Dumbleton Hall, especially at Christmas time and at special occasions in the year. He was tragically lost in a kayak accident at the age of just 25 – *'if he had lived,'* wrote Stanley Baldwin the Prime Minister *'he might have ranked ... amongst the greatest of Polar explorers.'*

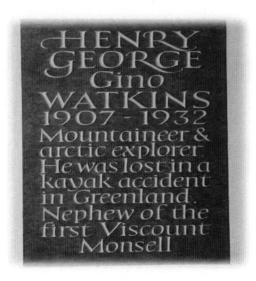

The memorial in the Church to Henry George 'Gino' Watkins FRGS – 29th January 1907- c20[th] August 1932

Gino Watkins:-courtesy of the Scott Polar Research Institute©

Henry was born in London and was educated at *Lancing College*; he early on in his life acquired a great love of exploration and mountaineering. He, as a child, had spent much time with his father and family on holidays spent in the Lake District, the Alps and the Tyrol. He was also interested in polar exploration, studied at Cambridge under *James Wordie* and organized his first expedition to Edgeøya, in the summer of 1927 at only 20 years of age.

Henry also learned to fly, and was one of the first members of the *Cambridge University Air Squadron.*

In 1928-29, he went on an expedition to Labrador and established a base at *North West River*; here he explored much of the previously unmapped territory. He he carried out probably his most important work with the *British Arctic Air Route Expedition* in 1930-31. He explored with a team of 14 men the east coast of Greenland and monitored the weather conditions for a proposed England to Winnipeg air route. He also at this time discovered the *Skaergaard intrusion* while on a 600 mile open boat journey around the southern coast of Greenland. For his work at this time he won the *Founders Medal* from the *Royal Geographical Society*, which brought him international fame.

The Founders Medal for the Royal Geographical Society©

Watkins next attempted to organize an expedition to cross Antarctica, but it was the time of the Great Depression and funds could not be found, so he returned to Greenland in 1932 with a small team to continue work on his air route expedition. On the 20th August he was hunting seals in a kayak in Tugtilik Fjord and did not return. Later that day his empty kayak was found floating upside down by his companions. His body was never found.

Henry George 'Gino' Watkins in his kayak

Henry Watkins is commemorated by the *'Gino Watkins Memorial Fund'* managed by the *Royal Geographical Society and the University of Cambridge*, which provides grants for polar exploration.

'Watkins Island' a sub-Antarctic island in the Southern Ocean, commemorates Watkins.

****

In the Church and dealt with in more detail later is a large painted monument to *Sir Charles Percy*, who was the son of the *Earl of Northumberland* and *Dorothy Cocks*, his wife. The colourful monument of two figures kneeling over their deceased child is quite thought-provoking.

The redundant *Church of St Mary's* in the nearby village of Washbourne is also in the parish of Dumbleton.

An early postcard of St Peter's Church, Dumbleton:-courtesy of the Dumbleton Society and the late Don Caisey©

It is more than likely that a Saxon Church was originally on the site of the present church, but this early church would more than likely have been built of wood and any remains have long since disappeared. The present Church shows signs of *Norman* and *Norman Transitional* and *Early English* work as is the style of Worcester Cathedral. The Church has been restored on various occasions and consists of: Chancel, Nave, Transept, South Aisle and a Western Tower.

The Nave: This is likely to be early Norman, around 1066-1100, and there are some traces of Saxon work around the base of the walls. The Nave has a clerestory to bring in light, but only one aisle. On the north wall of the nave a lancet window can be seen.

One of the early lancet windows in the Church: JRH – Christmas 2014©

The South Aisle: is a later addition and it can be seen that it does not reach to the west. It was added in the Perpendicular period c1370-1550, and contains some square-headed windows of two lights. The South aisle is divided from the Nave by two irregular shaped arches. These are supported by the Nave wall and a huge column in the centre, which was more than likely part of the Nave prior to this aisle being constructed.

The view of the Church looking down the Nave with the transepts on either side of the fine arch

An example of one of the square-headed windows of the clerestory which bring light into the Nave:-
JRH©

The Nave looking towards the back of the Church. Today there are plain white walls but in medieval times these walls would have been brightly painted:-JRH©

The Western Tower. This is the same date as the main body of the Nave, and it has two lancet windows. The belfry, a perpendicular addition contains 6 bells. The tower also holds a clock with two faces, one looking towards the village on the north side, and the other facing west towards Dumbleton Hall.

The Church Tower at St Peter's Dumbleton in 2015:- JRH©

The Nave looking through the second supporting arch towards the Choir and the East Window

The Church at Dumbleton and the Choir: - courtesy of the Dumbleton Society and the late Don Caisey©

The Chancel The majority of the windows in this part of the Church are perpendicular in style. There are two piscinas in the south wall of the Chancel. This was quite usual in the 13ᵗʰ Century when the Church may have contained various small chapels.

Three of the various piscinas in Dumbleton Church- the piscina would have contained Holy Water for blessings and for making the sign of the cross. These are found in most Catholic Churches. They are also used for rinsing away the water from the used chalice and paten after Communion:-JRH©

The North Transept described as the 'sepulchral chapel' or 'burial chapel', built for the Daston (various spellings) family. There is a window with two lights.

The Font: This is said to have been medieval, as often the font is the oldest part of the church, but this one is of 17th Century work and in one panel are the names of two Churchwardens, *Richard Ingles* and *Charles Agg,* and the date 1661. There is a wooden cover. At one time all font covers were locked to prevent witches stealing the Holy water! The base is of a different style, possibly Saxon in origin.

The stone font in St Peter's is dated 1661 but it may have been altered from a previous one, perhaps Norman or even earlier. The base on which the present font stands appears to be Saxon in origin. The font is used for holding the baptismal Holy water:-JRH©

248

The Church has been restored on numerous occasions including in 1873 and in 1906. The Church was reseated in 1905, and a new porch added, which holds a sundial and an inscription '*Waste me not*'. Roof repairs were carried out in 1969.

The Church porch and the sundial on the west door to the Church:-JRH©

The Grinall Wedding c1920s:- courtesy of the Dumbleton Society & the late Don Caisey©

Over the north door is a stone carving representing to the then superstitious congregation the devil and his 'branches of evil.' It is a form of '*Green Man*' which goes back to pagan times. Often Churches and Cathedrals had ugly and sometimes terrifying images over their doorways, on the corbels, called 'grotesques' or 'gargoyles,' to remind the people of their sins before they entered God's Holy House.

The North door at St Peter's & the carving of the devil and the branches of evil:-JRH©

The carving over the north door is of a strange figure whose identity has been variously interpreted. He may be the ancient fertility symbol, of the *'Green Man' with 'ears of an ass and three pieces of foliage springing from his mouth'* or the devil himself. In the early days of the twentieth century, the villagers called him the *'cat o' nine tails'*, whose presence was a warning to sinners entering the church to repent and pray for forgiveness before entering the Church itself. Whoever this feature represents his features are more amusing than fearful, his impish face surveying the north side of the churchyard, watching the graves in what was customarily regarded as the *'devil's domain.'* This is the shadowy north aspect discouraging people from being buried here, although at Dumbleton this does not appear to be the case, as the oldest graves appear to be the Jacobean table tombs which are evenly distributed around the churchyard. This was perhaps because the north side was the easier to access from the village itself.

Some of the decorated table tombs on the north side of the graveyard:-JRH©

An early family group probably about c1900:- courtesy of the Dumbleton Society & the late Don Caisey© They are all dressed in their Sunday best for a special occasion of some sort.

The induction of the new vicar of Dumbleton: - courtesy of the Dumbleton Society and the late Don Caisey©

The splendid timber roof of St Peter's Church. The nave roof was heightened in the 14th century to include a late Perpendicular clerestory which allowed much more natural light to enter the church.

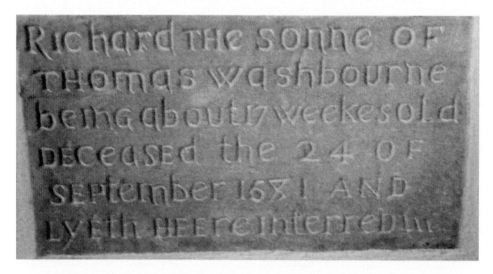

A moving memorial to Thomas Washbourne's young son, reminding us of the transience of life particularly in the 17th Century:-JRH©

The Memorials in the Church of St Peter's, Dumbleton

The Nave, North Wall

Frances, Lady Cocks, died 1723 – 1ˢᵗ wife of Sir Richard Cocks. 2ⁿᵈ Baronet (died 1726). Lady Cocks was the daughter of Richard Nevell.

Tablet to the men of Dumbleton, who lost their lives in the 1914-18 War.

Tablet to the men of Dumbleton, who lost their lives in the 1914-18 War by Norman Jewson, 1921

The Nave, South Wall

Tablet in memory of Rev. Robert Wedgwood, MA – Rector of the Parish from 1851-1881 (30 years)- he is spoken of with great affection by Ann Staight in her diary and Susan Oldacre has written about him too, in '*The Blacksmith's Daughter.*'

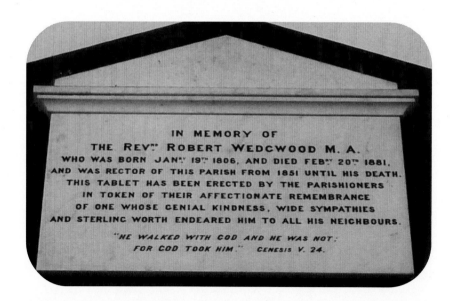

The Rev. Robert Wedgwood with his four daughters: from left, Annie (in riding habit), Eliza (crocheting?), Henrietta and Eleanor; below right the Rev. Allen Wedgwood, older brother of Robert: - courtesy of the 'Dumbleton Society' and the late Don Caisey© They were both grandsons of the famous potter Josiah Wedgwood. Allen came to live with his brother being an invalid, and he married in 1839 his first cousins, Emma Wedgwood and Charles Darwin, author of 'Origin of Species.' (1844)

The Rev. Robert Wedgwood's grave in the Churchyard: - JRH

Sir Robert Cocks died in 1765 – by a fall from a horse. He was the 4th and last Baronet and married Elizabeth, daughter of James Cholmeley.

Here is the Tablet in memory of Richard Clayton, who died in 1801 and the tablet in memory of his wife, Elizabeth who died in 1810 – Elizabeth, daughter died also in 1810.

South Aisle

Elizabeth – wife of Sir Robert Cocks, Baronet, daughter of James Cholmeley of Easton in the county of Lincoln. Memorial to her six children, five of whom died before her own death in 1749.

Marble monument to Miss Dorothy Cocks, who died in 1767 – Youngest and only surviving daughter of Sir Robert Cocks, 4th Baronet. Catherine her sister died after her mother in 1749 but before her father in 1765. Dorothy was 18 years of age.

Chancel, North Wall

Sir Charles Percy, his wife and child – Sir Charles died in 1628, his wife Dorothy died in 1646, their child Anne died before her father. Dorothy, daughter of Thomas Cocks of Cleeve, was formerly married to Edmund Hutchings.

258

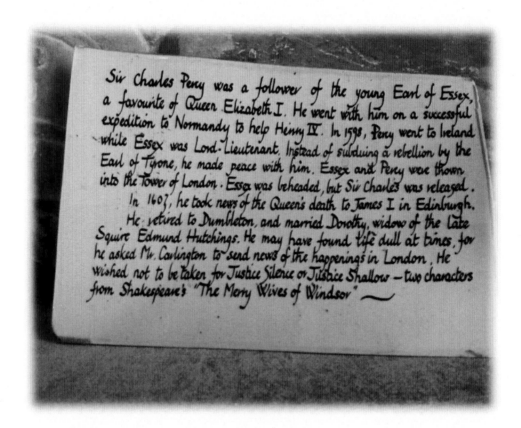

Sir Charles Percy was a follower of the young Earl of Essex, a favourite of Queen Elizabeth I. He went with him on a successful expedition to Normandy to help Henry IV. In 1598, Percy went to Ireland while Essex was Lord-Lieutenant. Instead of subduing a rebellion by the Earl of Tyrone, he made peace with him. Essex and Percy were thrown into the Tower of London. Essex was beheaded, but Sir Charles was released.

In 1603, he took news of the Queen's death to James I in Edinburgh.

He retired to Dumbleton, and married Dorothy, widow of the late Squire Edmund Hutchings. He may have found life dull at times, for he asked Mr. Carlington to send news of the happenings in London. He wished not to be taken for Justice Silence or Justice Shallow – two characters from Shakespeare's "The Merry Wives of Windsor" ~

Sir Richard Cocks, and Dame Susanna his wife – Sir Richard died in 1684 and his wife in 1689. Sir Richard was the ancestor of the Baronets of Dumbleton. He was the grandson of Thomas Cocks of Cleeve.

Charles Cocks died in 1654 – Bust. He was the son of Thomas Cocks of Cleeve, and died a bachelor. As other memorials display, the Dumbleton estate remained in the possession of the Cocks family until the latter half of the 18th century, while in the 19th century it was acquired by the Hollands.

Colin Ashwin, MA – He was born in 1870 and died in 1938, and was Rector of this Parish, 1904-38 (34years).

The Altar

The altar was erected by the children and fellow parishioners of Caroline Mary Sybil Eyres, Viscountess Monsell 1881-1959 in her memory.

The East Window

To the Glory of God and in loving memory of Henry William Eyres, born July 20th 1857, and who died in Naples on April 6th 1881. Erected by order of his wife, Caroline Isabel Eyres.

The Window on the South Wall

To the Glory of God and in loving memory of Anne Elizabeth Kettlewell, born November 22nd 1824 and died December 6th 1886. The East and the Sanctuary windows of 1887 are by *Hardmans of Birmingham* and the two light chancel north windows from 1947 are by *H. J. Stammers.*

The monument to Sir Richard Cocks 1684, a gilded Baroque stone monument, with black marble columns and several cherubs. It is a stylish local work, perhaps by *Reeve* of Gloucester

Swinton Colthurst Holland, who died in 1827 – also his wife Anne, who died in 1845

Edward Holland, who died in 1875 – Son of Swindon Colthurst Holland – Agnes Sylvia Holland, died in 1870

Agnes Sylvia Holland the granddaughter of Edward by his eldest son Edward Thurstan and Marianne Holland the daughter of the novelist Elizabeth Gaskell:-JRH©

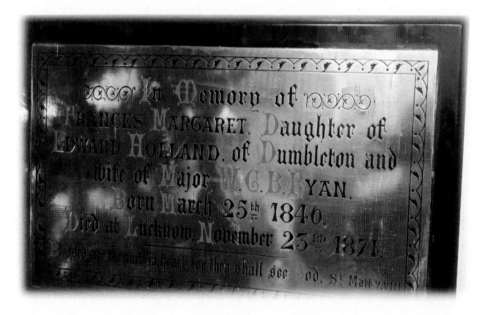

Frances Margaret Ryan, who died in 1874 – Daughter of Edward Holland

Frances was born at Dumbleton in 1846. In 1870 she married *Captain William Cavendish Bentinck Ryan* at Dumbleton. He served as an officer in the *Bengal Staff Corps* and was the son of Sir Edward Ryan, the *Chief Justice of the Supreme Court in Calcutta*.

Three children were born to Frances and William in India – *William Swinton Ryan* in July 1871, *Ernest Holland Ryan* in April 1873 and *Francie Margaret Ryan* in November 1874. Unfortunately, Frances Ryan died when giving birth to the youngest child. *Frances Margaret Ryan* was born and baptised on 23rd November 1874 and her mother died on the same day and was buried the next day. The baby must have been named in remembrance of her dead mother.

In 1881 Frances's husband, *William C.B. Ryan* was living in Charlton Kings, Cheltenham with his family and described as Colonel Retired List.

One of the saddest memorials in the Church is to Edward Holland's son Henry who died in 1871 aged just 11 years.

H.E. Holland, who died in 1871

In the 'Cheltenham Looker Out' for the 6th January 1872 was the following sad entry:

'*Deaths*

December 25th at Malta of diphtheria, Henry Ewan, son of Edward Holland in this county, aged 11 years.'

The tragic death of Henry Ewan would appear even more poignant as he died on Christmas Day so far from his home at Dumbleton.

Nearby is the memorial to Mary Jane Buddell, who died in 1826 and was the Wife of the Rev. Buddell. The fairly plain memorial in the shape of a heart is unusual.

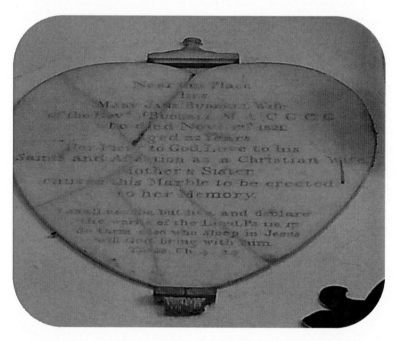

In the North Aisle on a flat stone were the figures of a man and a woman in brass (now disappeared).

*These were Robert Dasto*n (various spellings) and his wife Margaret. He died in 1513, descended from Saxon ancestry. This family were local landowners for many years.

Flat stones in the Nave: Anthony Best d.1687, Elizabeth Keen d. 1753. These are covered with carpet so cannot be viewed.

1260	Thomas	1850	Robert Wedgewood
1277	John	1881	Francis Willoughby Jones
1370	Walter Aston	1894	Charles Fairfax
1375	Reginald Pony	1904	Collins Ashwin
1406	John Knight	1938	J. Laughton
1530 - 35 -----		1940	William Tucker
1581	Oliver Diston	1952	R. Blakeway Phillips
1616	Nicholas Wallington	1958	W. Du-Pré
1641	Thomas Washbourne	1960	Norman Southgate
1687	Charles Cocks	1971	Eric Giles
1718	Thomas Baghott	1980	Peter Richards
1733	William Cocks	1994	Peter Smith
1734	Kinard Baghott	1995	Stanley Finch
1735	Thomas Baghott	2002	Clifford Poole
1762	John Baghott de la Bere	2009	Nick Carter
1795	John Still		
1797	William Lisle Bowles		
1822	Samuel Garrard		

Rectors of Dumbleton

There are three hatchments in the Church and Vestry- which are Coats of Arms indicating death in that particular family. These are often carried with the coffin. The hatchments are

269

for Charles Cocks, first Baron Somers, and c.1806. Also two in the vestry: Elizabeth Cocks c1749 and Swinton Colthurst Holland c1827.

1. *Swinton Colthurst* Holland who died in 1827- bought the Dumbleton Estate from the Cocks family.
2. *Elizabeth Cocks*, 2nd daughter of James Cholmeley of Easton. She married Sir Robert Cocks, 4th Baronet and died in 1749.
3. *Charles Somers*, 1st Baronet Somers (heir to the Cocks family), who died in 1806.
   - Readers of '*The Blacksmith's Daughter*' will find the Staights's tombstone in the Churchyard near the end wall of the North Transept.

There are 6 bells in the church tower which have the following inscriptions:

1. (Treble) '*Peace and Good Neighbourhood* 1729'
2. '*Prosperity to this Parish* 1729'
3. '*Prosperity to the Church of England*'
4. '*A. B. R. Rudhall cast us all in 1729*'
5. '*Rich'd Tyso and John Andrews Churchwardens 1729*'
6. (Tenor*)* '*I to the Church, the living call and to the grave so summon all 1729*'

Rev F S.Marshall 1869-1874	Rev Edward Whyly 1874-1893	Rev William Wilkinson 1893-1913
Rev A.W.Harper 1913-1929	Rev H.W.Bathhurst 1929-1936	Rev George Green 1936-1948
Rev W.L.Crutchley 1950-1955	Rev J.O.Johnson 1956-1961	Mr R.Cheaney 1961-1983

Some of the vicars of Dumbleton: - courtesy of 'The Dumbleton Society' & the late Don Caisey©

In the Churchyard

It is interesting to consider the great age of the Church and the Churchyard itself. Over the centuries many thousands of people must have been buried here, either inside the Church or in the graveyard close to its ancient walls. In past centuries most people, especially if they have had connections with the village would have wanted to be buried as close to the sanctity of the church as possible. Many graves would have had no marker, or just a wooden cross. It would be interesting to see if a map of the Churchyard has been kept through the centuries which could show us who is here.

There are many interesting tombstones, some so ancient they are impossible to read, but others are of interest.

Almost the first graves one sees on entering the churchyard, or on leaving the church by the north door, are a group, arranged irregularly in three rows, spanning two hundred years from 1763 to 1964. All commemorating members of the *Staight* family (various spellings), not far in fact from '*The Villa.*' There are other *Staight* graves on the south side of the Churchyard but these are mostly twentieth century ones. The *Staight Family* were the village blacksmiths and butchers and come alive in Susan Oldacre's wonderful book '*The Blacksmith's Daughter*'.

The book is a Victorian tale. Ann was born in 1855 and died in 1892. Her name is on the '*Staight*' tombstone in the churchyard. Her diaries have been the basis of the wonderful story Susan Oldacre has woven around this character. She is a personality brought vividly to life in a period of history very much removed from the present day. It was an era with greater opportunities in education and employment, with improved women's rights and rapid advances in medicine. Her life up until its final episode was quiet and contented and comfortable, for she was part of a large family circle and enjoyed a long and loving friendship in an unusually pleasant environment.

Apart from the book, there is no family folklore about her and no one living who knew her, but Susan Oldacre has brought her personality to life.

The diaries Ann kept, give us an insight into life at Dumbleton during the fascinating period of its history, when Edward Holland (1806-1875) was living at the Hall and much of the village had been remodelled by him to provide an excellent and comfortable environment and homes for his workers. Her picturesque village set amongst the orchards of the Vale of Evesham and backed by the hills of Cotswold and Bredon is still there, as is 'The Villa', home of three, possibly four, successive generations of Staight blacksmiths. This fascinating story is beautifully told and is one which will long live in the mind of those today who read it to get an insight into the Dumbleton of this time.

Ann sadly contracted nephritis, which is an inflammation of the kidneys. She was put on the train to enter the asylum in Gloucester. The medicine they gave at the time would have contained arsenic and in the diary Ann, mentions that she often finished off other people's medicines, which would not have helped with her early death at only 36.

The 'Villa' Front view of the villa and the view from the back and the adjoining blacksmith's smithy: courtesy of Mr and Mrs Irvine©

One of the 'Staight' gravestones. This is one of the many graves of the people of Dumbleton over the past centuries. The grave with all its names, gives us today a realisation of the transience of life. Diseases which today can be treated, in the 1800s could not; even flu, fairly common today, was a killer in this time. Tuberculosis or 'consumption' was another terrible ailment which took many lives. Ann herself died of nephritis and inflammation of the kidneys.

From the gravestone above here is Charles Pitman Staight, Master Blacksmith and 'Mayor of Dumbleton': his wife Ann and daughter Sarah:-courtesy of the Dumbleton Society and the late Don Caisey©

Sarah later married Leslie Legge of the mill at Dumbleton; this house later became the home in England of Patrick Leigh Fermor and his wife Joan, who was the daughter of Viscount Eyres-Monsell.

The Mill House and the Legge Brothers: - courtesy of the Dumbleton Society and the late Don Caisey©

276

Sarah with her daughters Nancy and Ruth Legge

In the middle row of the group, its headstone facing east towards the Hill, is one of the oldest, and certainly the most remarkable of the family group, an eighteenth century group, which has rated a mention in '*The Buildings of England*' as one of 'three' well preserved examples of a local type of excellent low relief headstones. Many of the gravestones in the Churchyard at Dumbleton are made of a local stone which has crumbled and so many are sadly illegible to the casual observer. At the top of the stone is a coat of arms containing three torches and three upturned horseshoes supporting on the one side a winged mythological figure and on the other side by a neatly bridled and saddled horse. These symbols mean that generations of blacksmiths were buried here.

The table tomb of Edward Holland who built Dumbleton Hall & the site of the family vault in January 2015.In the family vault with Edward are the following: Edward's mother who died in 1845, his first wife Sophia, who died in1851, his daughter, Susan Florence who died in 1852 and his granddaughter, Agnes Sylvia (Thurstan Holland's daughter).

The headstone on Edward Hollands grave:-JRH©

Joan and Patrick Leigh Fermor's graves in the Churchyard – Joan was the daughter of
Viscount Monsell:- JRH©

Henry Bolton Graham Eyres-Monsell, the brother of Joan (1912-2003), the Hon. Diana
Monsell (1907-1985) and Patricia Monsell (1918-1957)

The Times for the 26th July 1994 – '*Will to the Hon Henry Bolton Graham Eyres - Monsell 2[d] (and last) Viscount Monsell of Evesham of Dumbleton, Glos. Left an estate valued at £7,247,681 net.*

Henry Bolton Graham Eyres-Monsell (1905-1994) who was known as 'Graham' had an interesting career. He served during World War Two in the Intelligence Corps and reached the rank of Lieutenant Colonel. He was mentioned in dispatches on 16th September 1943 and recommended for the MBE for his services in the Intelligence Corps and particularly for his work in the planning stage of *Operation Torch*. He was also awarded the United States Medal of Freedom with Bronze Palm.

He became the 2nd Viscount Monsell on the death of his father, and on dying with no issue the title became extinct. (Whitaker's Almanack -1990)

The late 17th Century manor house of the Cocks family is thought to have stood just west of the church. It later became a farmhouse before total demolition in c1830. The 18th century brick stables further north partially survive, as the centre of a pleasant Neo-Georgian housing development of c1996 by *John Falconer Associates.*

Nutmeadow House, east of the church, is constructed of reconstituted stone Neo-Georgian of seven bays, by *Astam Design Partnership,* 1974, and stands on the site of the 19th century Neo-Tudor rectory by *Solomon Hunt* of Evesham.

Pictures of Dumbleton Village

In Dairy Lane, there is the brick Village Hall, with its central cupola, built for Mrs Eyres in 1899, and, at the west end, the former dairy and laundry, built in 1904 by *Kitson;* of roughcast, brick and narrowly set half-timbering. Its style has been imitated by another small housing development by *John Falconer Associates.*

The Dairy House: - courtesy of the Dumbleton Society and the late Don Caisey©

The Dairy House in January 2015:-JRH©

The Butcher's Shop in Dumbleton Village - c1890:- courtesy of the Dumbleton Society and the late Don Caisey© .This is Anne Staight's brother Joe from '*The Blacksmith's Daughter*'who left the blacksmith family at '*The Villa*' behind this cottage to train as a butcher in London and when he returned brought his bride Louisa Rose who with their children are shown in the photograph.

Joe's family: left Joe and Louise with Josie and Lily (1888); right, Pitman and Emma (1895):- courtesy of Susan Oldacre (Susan Sinnott) and 'The Blacksmith's Daughter' & Mr and Mrs Irvine from 'The Villa.'©

Louisa Rose. She had met Joe who was at the time living in North London training to be a butcher at Balham. She was in fact the 2nd daughter of a Surrey cattle dealer from the picturesque parish of Wotton near Dorking. Her mother's family had run the Wotton Hatch Inn (formerly called the Evelyn Arms after the Evelyn family who had lived at Wotton House – the most famous of the family being the 17th Century diarist John Evelyn):- Courtesy of Susan Oldacre (Susan Sinnott) & Mrs and Mrs F. Irvine of 'The Villa'©

View looking down the main street towards Edward Holland's Memorial: - courtesy of the 'Dumbleton Society' and the late Don Caisey©

Mr Bardy (?) in the village of Dumbleton: courtesy of the Dumbleton Society and the late Don Caisey©

A Dumbleton Village Family c1905: courtesy of the Dumbleton Society and the late Don Caisey©

A village picnic c1914-18:- courtesy of the Dumbleton Society & the late Don Caisey©

The V.A. Hospital at the Village Hall in Dumbleton:-courtesy of the Dumbleton Society & the late Don Caisey©

The Hall was built in 1899 and was given to the village by Mrs Eyre to celebrate the 21st birthday of her daughter, Sybil.

The plaque on the entrance to the Village Hall with the initials for Caroline, Isabel Eyres 1899:-
JRH©

An early photograph of the village hall, Dumbleton:-courtesy of Mrs Karen Morris and the Village Hall committee©

During the First World War it was used as a hospital for wounded servicemen and during the Second World War it became an annexe for the school, to give extra room for the influx of evacuees into the village.

Dumbleton Hospital in 1915:-courtesy of Mrs Karen Morris and the Village Hall Committee of Dumbleton Village Hall©

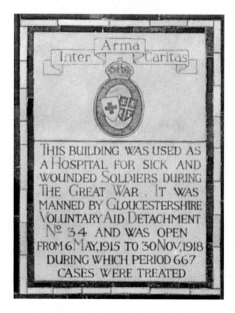

The plaque on the entrance door wall and a photograph of the Village Hall during the First World War:-courtesy of the Dumbleton Society and the late Don Caisey

The Village Hall today: - courtesy of the 'Dumbleton Society' & the late Don Caisey©

Christmas card sent during the First World War: - courtesy of the Dumbleton Society and the late Don Caisey©

Flower Stall at the Dumbleton Bazaar on 22nd April 1916:- courtesy of the Dumbleton Society & the late Don Caisey© This was part of the Dumbleton social year with celebrations hierarchical, horticultural and ecclesiastical. Ann in her Victorian diary mentions the celebratory birthday party of Miss Eyres at Dumbleton Hall. Although this was a children's tea party (and without a guest of honour, for Miss Eyres, at one year old, was not able to grace the proceedings with her presence), it gave Ann and the other young people in the village the chance to dress up: *'August 29 th. Put out silver ornaments ready to wear to tea party, tacked frilling in dress....'*

Ann Staight in her diary mentions going for an outing to the *Worcester Exhibition* (1882) and to the Cathedral. After the great success of the *Great Exhibition* in 1851, it was decided to have an exhibition in Worcester of a similar kind.

In 1882 the empty railway engine works was used as a showcase for the County's historical treasures and industrial and artistic endeavours. The exhibition was a colossal success; some 280,000 visitors came to view it in the three months it was on show. The profits from this exhibition were to be used to establish museums, libraries and other educational facilities in Worcestershire- (for a detailed look at the Worcester Exhibition and the life of John Corbett Vol.1 & 2 See John Hodges's Books)

'Lay till 6.30, dressed and went down lit fire, very misty. John proposed going to the Worcester Exhibition, so I got ready, and we rode from Wood to Beckford.' At Ashchurch they changed on to the Worcester line, and at Worcester headed straight for the Cathedral. Ann mentions a different outing which the villagers of Dumbleton and herself took for a change of scene visiting Hailes Abbey and Toddington Manor. Both fairly close and within riding distance of Dumbleton. Stratford also is close by and a legend states that Shakespeare would visit Dumbleton on occasions while out riding.

'The Gables'- Dumbleton Village, made up of four gabled semi-detached brick pairs of c1862, built for Edward Holland by *George Hunt* of Evesham to a prizewinning design (at the Yorkshire Agricultural Society in 1861) by *Richardson & Ross* of Darlington:-courtesy of the Dumbleton Society & the late Don Caisey©

The building materials in Dumbleton village reflect what would have been available at the time of their construction locally, as materials were only transported large distances for expensive, high status buildings. Buildings constructed from local materials with little or no decoration are referred to as *vernacular,* whilst those displaying fashionable decorative features and employing alien features are known as *polite.* The only surviving example of this style is the '*Old Rectory'.* The imposing front facade and much of the structure is seventeenth-century, but visible from the south side is its late sixteenth-century timber-frame core. In its time this would have been probably with the Church the most important building in the village.

Of the vernacular buildings, the earliest would have been timber-framed, with wattle and daub noggins (infill panels) and thatched roofs. Later during the seventeenth, eighteenth and the nineteenth century stone buildings became more widespread and also the use of brick as with Edward Holland's brickyard. The thatched roofs were replaced by flat clay tiles. Today there can be seen a considerable variety in roofing materials including stone slates, thatch, clay tiles, welsh slates, concrete tiles and reconstituted slate tiles.

The Dumbleton Brick Works

In the course of my research I was given some interesting information by Pam and Rob Miffin relating to the brickyard at Dumbleton:

'..after remodelling the Hall about 1837, Edward Holland decided to open up the brickyard to the north of the village in 1850 to provide bricks for his plans to rebuild the village. There was an abundance of clay on the lower slopes of the hill and it was there he started the brickyard.

An example of a 'Dumbleton' brick: courtesy of Rob and Pam Miffin©

William Taylor was a brick burner by trade. He had come from the Claxton area of Norfolk with his family to manage the brickyard for Edward Holland. We presume they arrived prior to the opening of the yard in c1850, and they were certainly there on the 1851 census.

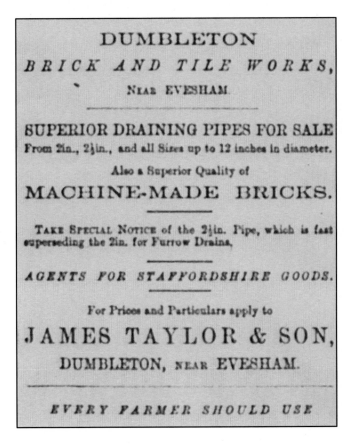

DUMBLETON
BRICK AND TILE WORKS,
NEAR EVESHAM

SUPERIOR DRAINING PIPES FOR SALE
From 2in., 2½in., and all Sizes up to 12 inches in diameter.

Also a Superior Quality of

MACHINE-MADE BRICKS.

TAKE SPECIAL NOTICE of the 2½in. Pipe, which is fast superseding the 2in. for Furrow Drains,

AGENTS FOR STAFFORDSHIRE GOODS.

For Prices and Particulars apply to

JAMES TAYLOR & SON,
DUMBLETON, NEAR EVESHAM.

EVERY FARMER SHOULD USE

The site of the Brickyard at Dumbleton: - courtesy of Pam and Rob Miffin©

William ran the yard along with his three sons, Samuel, James and William. James eventually became the sole owner after the death of his father William and his brother Samuel. Samuel ran the coal yards along with his brother William and Pam's other great, great grandfather. William Hawker (married to Betsy Taylor) was the manager, while the brickyard was left in time to James to run. After the death of William Snr and Samuel, William Jnr left the village to live in Bristol, leaving James owning all the business.

Samuel died the year after Edward Holland in 1876; it is possible that James acquired the brickyard after the death of Edward.

The brickyard had been sold by 1900 and the cottages that had been home to the Taylor family became the home of the Beasley family.

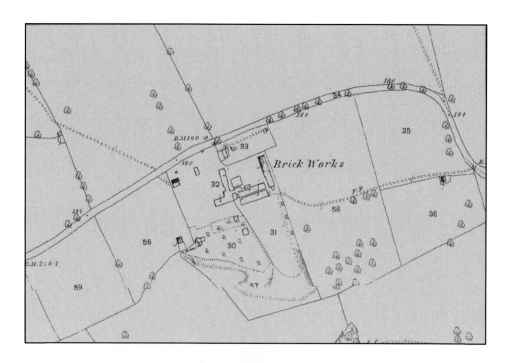

The Miffin family Cottages: courtesy of Rob and Pam Miffin©

This is quite a complex story, but as a family they were successful, taking full advantage of the railways to sell the bricks, tiles, coal and even salt, all thanks to their relationship with Edward Holland. Samuel Taylor named one of his sons Swinton after Edward Holland's father and son.

294

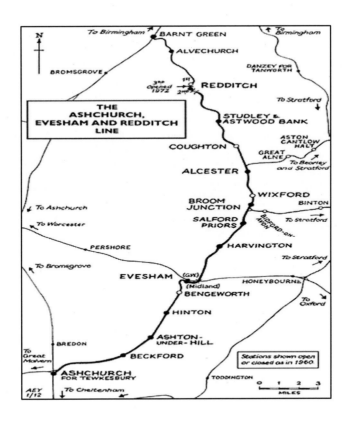

William Taylor Snr is Pam's great, great, great grandfather. William Hawker was her great great grandfather. In the photo of the shed with James Taylor brick and coal, we think the man in the doorway is William Hawker and the man holding the bike is Benjamin Taylor (son of James Taylor).'

Dumbleton Mill

Dumbleton Mill can be found one mile east of the village on the River Isbourne. This is an 18th-19th Century corn mill, brick with a stone dressing, two storeys plus two gables, and mullioned windows. There are pigeon holes in the end gables. The undershot cast iron wheel and the machinery is still *in situ.*

The Old Mill at Dumbleton: - courtesy of the late Don Caisey and the Dumbleton Society©

'The Gables'- Dumbleton Village in January 2015:-JRH©

'Ivy Cottage':- courtesy of the late Don Casey and the Dumbleton Society©

'Ivy Cottage' in January 2015:-JRH

'The Palaces', Dumbleton, is a compact group of four cottages of c1905, again by *Sydney Kitson*, with fine ashlar detailing; H-plan, with hipped end roofs, and brick chimneys. Detached washrooms at the rear: - courtesy of the Dumbleton Society and the late Don Caisey©. So named after the comments made by Lady Eyres-Monsell that these new houses for their workers on the estate were more like a palace than workers' cottages.

'The Palaces' in January 2015:-JRH©

300

Mr Kim Finch outside his cottage, the former Baker's Cottage in Dumbleton;-JRH©

No 39 Main Street - The Old Baker's Cottage showing the built -in Baker's oven: - courtesy of Mr Kim Finch, January 2015©

The Inglenook fireplace at No 39 with the old Baker's oven:-courtesy of Mr Finch in January 2015

Early postcard c1905 of Dumbleton:-courtesy of the Dumbleton Society & the late Don Caisey©

The old Estate Office with its slate tiled roof in January 2015:-JRH©

The former Estate Office and old thatched cottages which have been demolished:-courtesy of the Dumbleton Society and the late Don Caisey© In the background is the memorial to Edward Holland.

The same view as the previous image, looking up the road to the fountain:-JRH©

Edward Holland Memorial and the High Street and present day shop and cafe in January 2015:-
JRH©

Dumbleton in the snow: courtesy of the Dumbleton Society and the late Don Caisey©

Detail of the former photograph showing two rather stern ladies in their Sunday best with fine hats:-
courtesy of the Dumbleton Society & the late Don Caisey©

307

The Village Café in January 2015:-JRH©

'Yew Tree Cottage':-courtesy of the Dumbleton Society and the late Don Caisey©

c17-c18 century thatched timber-framed Cottages in the main street in January 2015:-JRH©

'The Police House' in Dumbleton:-courtesy of the Dumbleton Society & the late Don Caisey©

DUMBLETON POST OFFICE, GLOS.

The former Post Office in Dumbleton: - courtesy of the Dumbleton Society & the late Don Caisey©

The Post Office in Dumbleton:-courtesy of the Dumbleton Society & the late Don Caisey©

The present house on the site of the former post office of Dumbleton in January 2015. This was the former home of the late Vic Hopkins who was the Cricket County player for Gloucestershire between 1934 and 1948:- JRH©

The Rectory in Dumbleton:-courtesy of the Dumbleton Society & the late Don Caisey© -The former home of the Rev. Wedgwood. This house is now demolished.

The Old Rectory and farm:-courtesy of the Dumbleton Society & the late Don Caisey©

The original Cricket Pavilion: - courtesy of the Dumbleton Society & the late Don Caisey©

The opening of the original cricket pavilion in c1884:-courtesy of the Dumbleton Society and the late Don Caisey©

Detail from the opening of the cricket pavilion:- courtesy of The Dumbleton Society & the late Don Caisey©

The mention of cricket at Dumbleton is important as the village has one of the finest and most picturesque pitches in England. The first firm evidence of cricket being played in the village by a village team is of matches at Toddington and Winchcombe in 1882 and the first match played at the ground in Dumbleton was a game against the Evesham Grammar School on 11th July 1885. On the strength of this evidence the Dumbleton Cricket Club celebrated its centenary in 1985.

'I think the reason the Cricket Club maintained its continuity from 1885 onwards,' wrote Mr R. C. Meadows in the club's Centenary Year Book, '..was because the Eyres-Monsell family always wanted cricket there and they always ran a cricket week once a year where the gentry played against the local team.' These Cricket Weeks continued at Dumbleton until about 1935.

The cricket ground was once surrounded by elm trees, but these have disappeared as have most of this species in Gloucestershire due to Dutch elm disease, but the fine setting of the present club still remains today. There is still a keen and enthusiastic interest for the club in the village and the fine clubhouse is the venue for many of the village events not just for the cricket ones.

One famous member of the club was Vic Hopkins, the famous wicketkeeper who went from Dumbleton to Lords, where he played for the first of 139 matches for Gloucestershire. He was a county player between 1934 and 1948.

The village at the opening of the cricket pavilion: - courtesy of the Dumbleton Society & the late Don Caisey©

The cricket pavilion in January 2015- overlooking one of the finest cricket fields in England:-JRH©

The rear of the modern cricket pavilion overlooking a small lake: - JRH©

The weathervane on the bell tower of the modern pavilion- there are several of these interesting weathervanes around the village.

The Village School at Dumbleton:-JRH©

The Village School in 2015

The children of Dumbleton School c50s or 60s: courtesy of the Dumbleton Society & the late Don
Caisey & with permission from the present school 'Oak Hill' Primary©

Some other children from Dumbleton (date unknown):-courtesy of the Dumbleton Society & the late Don Caisey and with permission from Oak Hill Primary School©

Chapter Eight: The Post Office Fellowship of Remembrance

The Post Office Fellowship of Remembrance, who bought *Dumbleton Hall* in 1959, is a unique organisation with an interesting history all of its own. Its origins began with the initiative by GPO employees in the north-west of England between the two World Wars. This organisation made the decision to purchase property for the Post Office employees and their families to use for holidays and convalescence as a living memorial to their fellow workers who had died during the conflicts of the *First World War* and the *Second World War.*

It is an act of commemoration to those who gave their lives in the two world wars, providing and maintaining hotels for convalescent, holidays and for educational purposes.

All GPO and successive organisation employees are eligible for the membership, and members pay an annual subscription.

Convalescence was especially important bearing in mind the legacy of the First World War and the horrific injuries both mental and physical which were its epitaph. The organisation first took form as the *'Bryn Asaph'* movement, so called after their first property purchased in North Wales.

'Bryn Asaph' in North Wales: - Courtesy of Martin Grafton and the Post Office Fellowship of Remembrance©

Although supported by GPO management and considerable trade union involvement, the organisation remained completely independent.

As membership numbers and support grew within the GPO, the organisation expanded and in 1937 they bought *'Friars Carse'* in Dumfries, Scotland, a country house estate with close associations with Robbie Burns. Along with farms and a market garden, it also had a mile or so on the River Nith. The facilities were very much of their time, with matrons in charge, giving the emphasis on convalescence as well as holidays.

Friars Carse, Auldgirth. Dumfries, Scotland: - courtesy of the Post Office Fellowship of Remembrance© (see colour plate)

Developments were suspended by the advent of war again in 1939, although records show that the market garden at *Friars Carse* provided large quantities of food including much bottled fruit which no doubt helped with the catering and the rationing during the war.

The end of the war meant a renewed sense of purpose for the remembrance organisation. Its membership, organisation and property portfolio expanded into the 1950s. During this period the POFR membership grew to over 150,000, bringing in enough business to fully occupy the expanded number of centres and keeping the organisation as a 'members only' facility. A Board of Directors was appointed in part by the General Post Office, some by the Trade Unions and some elected by members of the company, supported by House Committees and a range of volunteers with the staff required to run the actual hotels.

At one time the Fellowship owned the following properties around Great Britain where convalescence would be available free, or where members could stay for a holiday. These included: *Bryn Asaph, St Asaph*, North Wales; *Friars Carse*, Dumfries; *Bushridge Hall*, Godalming, Surrey; *Knappe Cross,* Exmouth, Devon; *Waterhead*, Coniston, Lancashire; and **Dumbleton Hall,** on the Worcester Gloucestershire border.

The Fellowship also ran two family holiday centres at *Ledge Point* at Westgate on Sea and at the *Brighton Hydro* in Blackpool.

'Ledge Point' at Westgate on Sea: - courtesy of the Post Office Fellowship of Remembrance©

In the 1990s a fundamental change was made to the Organisation in order to sustain a viable hotel business, for its reduced membership no longer brought in the volume of trade or revenue required to run so many properties, so the Fellowship sold off some properties to help balance the finances. Today the remaining Post Office Fellowship of Remembrance properties are run by *Classic Hotels* and include **Dumbleton Hall** a traditional 19th century Manor House set in 19 acres of gardens with its own private lake. The hotel has stunning views of the Vale of Evesham and across to the Cotswolds.

Dumbleton Hall opened on the 1st August 1959, and the ceremony was performed by *Mr S. Donald Sargent C.B.* The matron appointed was a Miss E. F. Clarke. The accommodation comprised of a variety of guest bedrooms with dining facilities. Dumbleton Hall was the largest of the holiday centres owned by the Fellowship. The new centre had no licence for selling alcohol and it was not until June 1974 that a bar was first opened for the use of the residents.

Dumbleton Hall in the spring with the masses of daffodils: - courtesy of Mr Simon Kelly of Dumbleton Hall© (see colour plate)

In October 1996 it became one of the three country hotels in the '*P & T Classic Hotels*' chain and with a rolling two million pound enhancement programme started a new lease of life as a conference centre, restaurant and hotel and opened to the general public for the first time.

With the transition to '*Classic Hotels,*' the Board decided that the remaining three Hotels, *Dumbleton Hall, Waterhead,* at Coniston and *Friars Carse* in Dumfries would make a commercial unit that could be developed for the members but also cater for a wider customer base to meet the rising expectations of the increasingly competitive 21ˢᵗ Century leisure market.

Business plans and the management to deliver what was required in often demanding circumstances came to fruition under Gavin Dron's leadership. Gavin is an experienced hotel professional whose flair and enthusiasm are vital in moving the hotel chain forward. There is now an ongoing programme of enhancement of all the hotel facilities. At Dumbleton in particular 'Front of House' Dexter Cairns leads a dedicated team of enthusiastic people with panache and flair, among them the longest serving employee Kate Bryant, who has seen many managers come and go and enormous and beneficial changes at Dumbleton leading to many thousands of satisfied and happy guests to the hotel.

One of the other changes over recent years was to incorporate the *Post Office Fellowship of Remembrance* Head Office into Dumbleton Hall itself, and this brought a new 'Company Secretary,' Simon Kelly who has professionally tackled the huge range of tasks that his job description covers and many more tasks beyond that.

Simon has been supported most ably by the hotel 'engineer' director Mr Brian Fox. Both men have seen dramatic changes such as the new 'Bio Mass' boilers which have proved so much more economical and efficient than the old aging oil fired boilers. This idea has also been incorporated in the Classic Hotel's other sites at '*Waterhead*' and at '*Friars Carse.*'

Friars Carse with wedding marque: - courtesy of Classic Hotels©

Friars Carse is a country hotel in Auldgirth, Dumfries. '*Friarkerse*' was originally established as a friary back in the 13th century, close to the present '*Friars Carse.* The property became the home to the Riddell family and named '*Glenriddell*' with Rabbie Burns, as a regular house guest. The property extends to 45 acres extending to the banks of the River Nith.

The property passed through many different hands becoming home to Sir James Crichton (better known as Admiral Crichton) in 1809. The house was re-modelled in 1873, being once more renamed as '*Friars Carse*' in 1895, and established as a hotel in 1938.

'Waterhead' at Coniston in the Lake District, was where Sir Malcolm Campbell stayed with his young son Donald, when he broke the world water speed record in 1936.

Waterhead Hotel, Coniston, Cumbria:-courtesy of Classic Hotels©

A Unique Legacy

The unique legacy of the *Post Office Fellowship of Remembrance* was crystallised in 1957 when the two *Books of Remembrance* containing the names of the GPO employees killed in the two world wars of the 20th Century were dedicated in the presence of the Queen Elizabeth, the Queen Mother and became a priceless record in the trust of the Fellowship.

The two books of remembrance held by the Post Office Fellowship of Remembrance contain a total of 12,850 names of those Post Office employees who died in the First and Second World Wars:

From the First World War – 8,858 names and from World War II - 3,972 names, all of whom were GPO employees killed in these conflicts. *The Post Office Fellowship of Remembrance* was established as a living memorial providing holiday/convalescence for Post Office employees, but its most sacred and serious responsibility is the stewardship of these books which have a unique importance and a priceless value far beyond any monetary consideration.

The books were handwritten by a Post Office employee, *Mr J. A. Trezies* over a period of three years and unveiled by Her Majesty the Queen Mother at a dedication service in 1957.

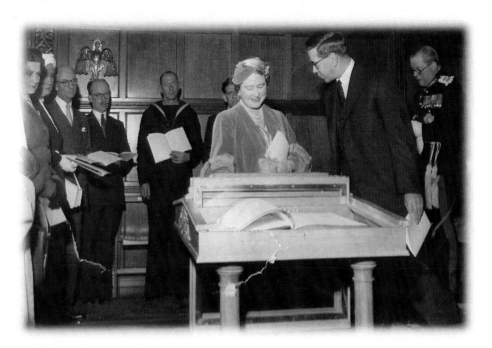

The Queen Mother dedicating the Books of Remembrance in 1957:- courtesy of Mr Martin Grafton©

Of the thousands of names listed, each one is unique. The names written down in the books, display their own names, the post office organisation where they were employed, military decorations and their branch of military service. The books do not give the rank or titles, as all the names are equal having made the same sacrifice in the two great conflicts of the 20th Century.

James Arthur Henry Trezies – 1905-1993

I would like to thank Mr Tim Peacock of Derby for the following information concerning James Trezies and his work on the Books of Remembrance:

'James Trezies was employed, in his teenage years as a boy messenger. He spent most, if not all of his career in the employ of the Post Office.

James was able to obtain a two year secondment in order to write, illustrate and bind in two *Books of Remembrance*, the Post Office's Roll of Honour for the two world wars. The books were 'finished' (lettering and tooling) professionally.

The books were 'unveiled' on 2^d April 1957 by the Queen Mother at Busbridge House. The House had been purchased by the Post Office Fellowship of Remembrance in 1951.

In the photographs the Queen Mother is using a quill pen. It would have been pens of this type, crafted by James, which would have been used in the writing of the books. The example in the photograph would have been cut and prepared by 'Uncle Jim'.

The Queen Mother using James Trezies's quill pen: - courtesy of Mr Tim Peacock©

Mr and Mrs Trezies admiring the completed books with the Queen Mother's unique signature: - courtesy of Mr Tim Peacock©

Faith and Jim Trezies: - courtesy of Mr Tim Peacock©

One of the invitations for the unveiling of the Books of Remembrance in 1957 in the presence of Her Majesty the Queen Mother: - courtesy of Mr Martin Grafton©

The unique display cabinet constructed specifically to house the Books of Remembrance: courtesy of Martin Grafton – archivist©

The Queen Mother at the Dedication of the Books of Remembrance in 1957 with the Postmaster General, Ernest Marples: - courtesy of Mr Martin Grafton©

The Books of Remembrance

The two books of Remembrance. One holds the 1914-18 names of the 8,858 men and women who lost their lives and the second book holds the 3,792 names of those of the General Post Office who lost their lives in World War Two:-JRH©

The Remembrance books are divided alphabetically, with each letter being beautifully illustrated with flowers for the First World War and trees for the second. Each name is lovingly and respectfully written on each page:

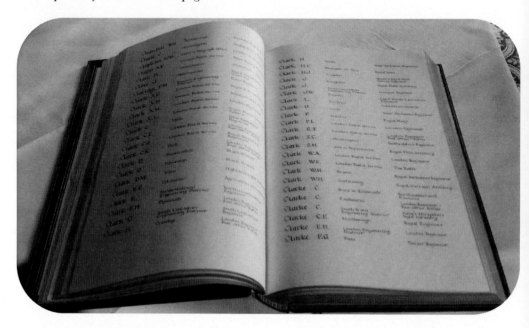

One of the pages from the Books of Remembrance:-courtesy of Mr Martin Grafton-Archivist©

The artwork in the books is worthy of further display and the following pages show examples from each of the books.

An example of the beautifully painted letters in the First World War Remembrance Book: - courtesy of
Mr Martin Grafton© (see colour plate)

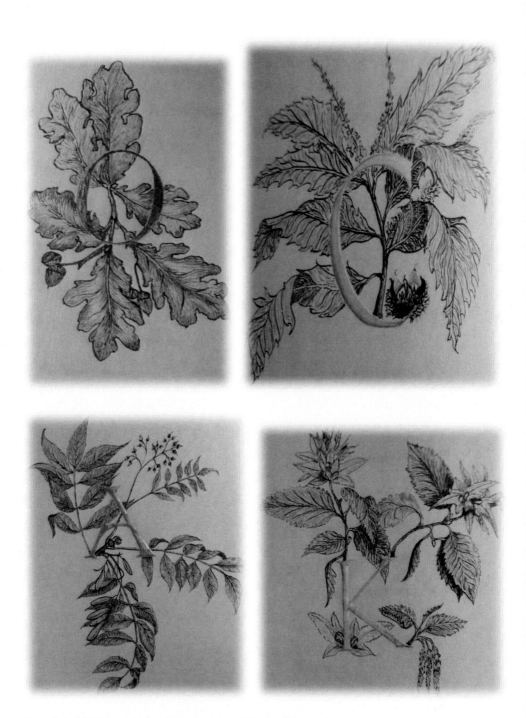

Examples of the letter paintings from the Second Book of Remembrance for the Second World War which features trees: - courtesy of Mr Martin Grafton© (See colour plates)

The Garden of Remembrance

At Dumbleton itself a Remembrance Garden was created and opened on 18th June 2001 to celebrate the 50th Anniversary of the Founding of the Post Office Fellowship of Remembrance.

The Remembrance Garden at Dumbleton Hall planted by the previous Post Office Fellowship of Remembrance Chairman Mr Pat Redrup and his wife Christine

Part of the Post Office Fellowship of Remembrance legacy is a fine piano which was one of three donated by the *Post Office Music Society* in 1953, in memory of *Kathleen Ferrier*, the contralto singer who died tragically in 1953 at the young age of 41 at the height of her career.

Kathleen Mary Ferrier (1912-1953) was an English contralto singer who in her life achieved an international reputation as a recording artist, concert and stage artist with a repertoire extending from popular ballads and folk songs to classical works of Bach, Mahler, Elgar and Brahms.

Her sudden death from cancer was a real shock for the public, who had come to love and enjoy Kathleen's singing, especially through the traumatic years of the Second World War, when her appearances acted as a huge morale boost for the people of this country and around the world. The shock was doubly poignant in that the public had no idea that she had been ill as she had kept her cancer a secret until after her death. She was at the height of her career which made her demise even more tragic.

Kathleen was the daughter of a Lancashire village schoolmaster, and early on in her life demonstrated her talent as a pianist, and won numerous amateur piano competitions while she worked as a telephonist with the General Post Office.

Her father's impending retirement and the subsequent fall in the family income meant Kathleen was denied the chance to attend a music college and in August 1926 she left school to start work as a trainee at the GPO telephone exchange in Blackburn. She did not however give up her music and her passion for the piano, and continued her studies under Frances Walker. In November 1928 she became the regional winner in a national contest for young pianists, organised by the Daily Express. Although she was not successful in the London finals she did win a Cramer upright piano. On 10th March 1929 she appeared as an accompanist at a concert in King George's Hall.

King George's Hall - Blackburn

On the 3rd July 1930 she was invited by the BBC at their Manchester studios to perform a short radio recital, playing works by Brahms and Percy Grainger. It was around this time that her training at the telephone exchange ended and she became a fully fledged telephonist with the General Post Office.

In 1931 at the age of 19, she passed her Licentiate examinations to the *Royal Academy of Music.* She now also took singing lessons to improve her voice and performance.

Early in 1934 she transferred into the GPO to the Blackpool telephone exchange and took lodgings nearby, to be close to her new boyfriend, a bank clerk named Albert Wilson. While in Blackpool she auditioned for the new 'Speaking Clock' service which the GPO was just introducing. Unfortunately she was not chosen for the final in London. Her decision in 1935 to marry Albert meant the end of her employment with the GPO, as at this time the organisation did not employ married women. Of her career to this point, the music biographer wrote of her:

'For more than a decade, when she had been studying music with the best teachers, learning English literature and foreign languages, acquiring stagecraft and movement skills, and travelling to London regularly to see opera, Miss Ferrier was actually answering the telephone, getting married to a bank manager and winning tinpot competitions for her piano playing.'

In 1942 her career was boosted when she met the conductor *Malcolm Sargent*, who recommended her to the influential '*Ibbs and Tillet*' concert management agency. She became a regular performer at leading London and country venues and made numerous BBC radio broadcasts.

She made her stage debut in the Glyndebourne Festival premier of Benjamin Britten's opera 'The Rape of Lucretia'. Kathleen built up excellent working relationships with other musical figures, including Britten, Sir John Barbirolli, Bruno Walter and the accompanist Gerald Moore.

She became internationally recognised and admired with her three tours of the United States between 1948 and 1950. She made many visits to Europe to sing and to play her favourite instrument the piano.

Kathleen in 1948 with her unique signature

Kathleen was diagnosed with breast cancer in the March of 1951. In between periods of hospitalisation and treatments she continued to perform and record. Her final public appearance was as 'Orfeo,' at the Royal Opera House in February 1953, just eight months before she tragically passed away. Among her memorials which included the three pianos donated including the one at Dumbleton were the *Kathleen Ferrier Cancer Research Fund* which was launched in the May of 1954 and the *Kathleen Ferrier Scholarship Fund,* administered by the *Royal Philharmonic Society,* which has since 1956 made annual awards to aspiring young professional singers the world over. (Thanks for the support of Martin Grafton – archivist for Dumbleton Hall and to Winifred Ferrier who wrote an incredible and moving biography of Kathleen Ferrier.)

The Kathleen Ferrier Memorial Piano at Dumbleton Hall:-JRH

Kathleen Ferrier's memorial service took place at Southwark Cathedral on the 14th November 1953. The Bishop of Croydon in his eulogy said of Kathleen's voice 'She seemed to bring into this world radiance from another world'.

In the very moving biography of her sister, *Winifred Ferrier* helps bring the life and work of a very special lady to life, I only wish after reading *'The Life of Kathleen Ferrier'* that I had known her.

Kathleen's father was a schoolmaster in Kathleen's home village close to Blackburn in Lancashire. Winifred gives a marvellous description of their father William:

'William Ferrier's life as a village schoolmaster suited him well. Although he had been brought up in the streets of a manufacturing town, he soon learned to identify every flower and bird to be seen for miles around Higher Walton. There was a real bond of affection between him and the sturdy, well-cared for school children, with whom he spent many happy hours wandering around the fields and lanes.'

Kathleen as born on the morning of the 22nd April 1912, it must have seemed strange to her later in life to think she was born just a week after the terrible *'Titanic'* disaster of the 15th April that year.

Later in her life Winifred takes periods of interest in the life of her sister, as when she first sang in Westminster Abbey in May 1943 in the middle of the Second World War when her voice brought so much comfort and enjoyment to those at home awaiting news of their loved ones away fighting the war against Hitler. It was at this time that she first sang many of the works with which her name was to become associated. When she was offered an engagement to sing a work unknown to her, she tried it through, accepting if it suited her voice. She relied on being able to learn it by the time the concert was due.

She travelled and enjoyed performing in the United States. In January 1948 she was on board *R.M.S. Mauretania* one of the most luxurious passenger ships of the period. She writes with such obvious enjoyment:

'Cunard White Star,
R.M.S. Mauretania,   Tuesday 6th January 1948

Dearest Win,

Hello, love! Here I am, propped up in bed, having a gorgeous breakfast and feeling the complete diva. Heavens, I never expected to enjoy this trip so much. We've had sunshine, gales and heavy swells and I've never turned a hair – even when I have seen other folks in distress!

I don't know where to start, but our main conversation is food! I have never seen such dishes and we are being spoiled by the chief steward who think up meals for us, so that we start with tomato juice, caviar with all the trimmings, soup, fish, lobster or salmon, beef steaks, joints of all descriptions, and the most amazing sweets ever. Baked ice-cream – that is ice-cream on cake with meringue all round it, or ice-cream with cherries in brandy, and the brandy lit with a match till there are blue flames all over it. Oh dear, I keep thinking about your struggling to make the joint spin out, but I'll send some parcels when I arrive – then you can both have a tuck in.

The R.M.S. Mauretania in 1938

The splendid dining room on board the Mauretania

Arriving in New York, she wrote:

'What a city – it is just a fairyland of good things and wonderful buildings, and all the time I am wishing you could both be here to share these excitements and pleasures....................'

Kathleen also travelled on board both the *Queen Mary* and the *Queen Elizabeth* and obviously enjoyed travelling by ocean liner. This was the great age of the liners, with the *Queen Mary* travelling to New York and the *Queen Elizabeth* crossing its route on the way back to England. It was an exciting time after the terrible deprivations of the War.

The Queen Mary & the Queen Elizabeth

In 1948 she arrived in New York on board the Queen Mary, and the ship was thirty-six hours late. So Kathleen went straight from the ship to the rehearsal of a concert version of 'Orfeo'. She was to sing it at the Town Hall, New York with Ann Ayars, her Euridice of the previous Glyndebourne season, and was looking forward very much to meeting her again. The role of 'Orfeo' was her favourite.

While in New York, Kathleen rehearsed with *Arpad Sandor*, the accompanist who was to go on tour with her. To her great joy she also managed to fit in a lesson with *Bruno Walter*. A few days later began a very strenuous tour.

At Christmas 1949 Kathleen was on board the '*Queen Elizabeth*,' bound for America again. She was looking forward with pleasure to this tour; there would be many happy reunions with many good friends. Sadly Kathleen's cancer was getting worse. After being in hospital for extended periods she told her nurse that *'Wouldn't it be lovely if I could go to sleep and not wake up again.'* On the morning of the 8th October 1953 she died peacefully.

The charming sitting room in the Dumbleton Hall Hotel, with Kathleen Ferrier's memorial piano in pride of place – 2015:-JRH©

* *

In completing the book on Dumbleton Hall Mr Martin Grafton the archivist whose support has been extremely important in the writing of this book has written a brief conclusion to finish off the History of Dumbleton Hall and the village:

To conclude, this book brings together so many memories, Martin Grafton's archives, the late Don Caisey and Adrian Philip's splendid collection of photographs, the records of the 'Dumbleton Society', village stories including Susan Oldacre's book *'The Blacksmith's Daughter,'* which Susan has given permission to use and quote from and a dash of English History.

In addition to the *Books of Remembrance*, the *Post Office Fellowship of Remembrance* continues its support for 'Remembrance' in the 21ˢᵗ century. At the *National Memorial Arboretum* in Staffordshire and subscribing in its name, one of the engraved paving stones which will be laid in *'Heroes Square'* as part of the World Centre of Remembrance is now being planned at the *National Memorial Arboretum.*

Similarly for the nationally important *Books of Remembrance*, it is hoped that they will find their final home as part of a permanent display at the *Postal Museum* in London.

Likewise *Classic Hotels* will progress further into the 21ˢᵗ century, offering the best of wedding, conference, and holiday and dining venues. *'Friars Carse'* in Scotland, offers river fishing and another fine wedding venue increasing this tradition of fine hospitality, and contributing to the *Burns Hermitage* whose restoration the company has supported so well.

The Classic Hotel's other hotel, *'Waterhead'* on Coniston water has supported the local museum's plans to bring Donald Campbell's restored *'Bluebird'* back to the Lakes, and now has a Bistro bar and its own jetty at the waterside with views over to Ruskin's *'Brantwood.'*

* *

Acknowledgements for Dumbleton Hall

Grateful thanks must go to the staff and Manager Mr Gavin Dron and Simon Kelly at Dumbleton Hall for making me always welcome and to Mr Martin Grafton the archivist and one of the Directors of the *Post Office Fellowship of Remembrance* who has given his time and the free use of all his records and research material which have been of such importance in the research into the history of Dumbleton Hall. Without his support and enthusiasm for this project, this book would not have been written.

Grateful thanks is given for the encouragement and support of the Board of the Post Office Fellowship of Remembrance CIC owners of Dumbleton Hall. To the Chairman Mr Alan Bealby, Vice Chairman Ms Jenny Cole, Mr Martyn Bunn, Mr Tom Daffurn, Mr Ernie Dudley, Mr Brian Fox, Mr Martin Grafton, Mr Paul Mason, Debbie Terry and Company Secretary Mr Simon Kelly.

I wish to thank Mrs Sue Campbell for all her support and encouragement for this project, for all the valuable research she has carried out for me, for correcting the text and for finding all sorts of interesting articles and features which have contributed to this book and I hope made it so much more interesting.

To Mrs Jane Cox my proofreader who has patiently sorted and corrected my many peccadilloes into some sort of logical order- thank you Jane as without your help and much valued support this book would not have reached the printing stage.

To Mr Adrian Phillips who used to live in the *Old Rectory* in Dumbleton and being the head of the *Dumbleton Society* is a fountain of knowledge about the village and the Hall. Who has most kindly helped to read through the chapters of this book and correct my peccadilloes- for this I am most grateful.

Mrs Don Caisey who has given me permission to use her late husband's enormous collection of photographs and records alongside the Dumbleton Historical Society collections to illustrate this book, and the pictures which many people will enjoy. I have used photographs from the collections in most of the chapters in this book.

Chapter One – The Early History of Dumbleton

The corrections and proofreading of the early chapters by Mr Adrian Phillips has been very much appreciated as it is important to get the complicated and very long history of Dumbleton as accurate as we can make it - thank you Adrian for your support, encouragement and invaluable contributions to this book.

I have referred to a variety of sources for the early chapters which have included references to the following documents:

Sir Thomas Pope: An article which incorporates text from a publication now in the public domain: Chisholm, Hugh, ed. (1911). Encyclopaedia Britannica (11th ed.) Cambridge University Press.

POPE, Thomas (1506/7) of Clerkenwell, London and Tittenhanger, Herts – History of Parliament online. Retrieved 2012-07-10.

Edmund Hutchings - the nephew of Sir Thomas Pope:

Number XXV. Account of the first President, Fellows and Scholars of Trinity College, Oxford, nominated by Sir Thomas Pope, and admitted May 30th 1556. And of such others as were afterwards nominated by the same Authority – First Scholars.

Reference to Robert of Mortimer – reference: ChCP: Vol VI (453), Vol IX (256-264), Vol XII/2 (957-960);AR: Line 98 (31-32). Line 177 (2-3).

COCKS, Sir Richard, 2nd BT. (c1659-1726), of Dumbleton, Glos: 'The History of Parliament: The House of Commons -1690-1715. Ed. D. Hayton and E. Cruickshanks 2002.

Chapter Two – The First Dumbleton Hall

Dumbleton Old Hall- 'Park and Gardens'- Record id:4208.

With thanks to Charlotte Moody the Events and Office Administrator on behalf of James Hervey Bathurst for allowing me to use their portraits of the 1st Earl Somers by Romney & by John Harrison from the Eastnor Castle Collection.

Reference for the notes on Lord Somers: G. E. C., ed. Geoffrey F. White. 'The Complete Peerage.' (London: St. Catherine Press, 1953) Vol. XII, Part 1, p. 32.

Westbury Court Garden photographs:-courtesy of the National Trust and Ann Davies the Business Support Officer and Jerry Green the Gardener in Charge at Westbury Court-with grateful thanks.

Chapter Three – The Present Dumbleton Hall and Edward Holland

With thanks to Lorna Parker –Archivist at the Royal Agricultural University in Cirencester for her very much appreciated support in researching this chapter on Edward Holland and his connection with the University.

'The History of the Royal Agricultural College' Cirencester by Roger Sayce – 1992.

With grateful thanks to Susan Oldacre (Mrs R. G. Sinnott) for allowing me to take extracts from her splendid book 'The Blacksmith's Daughter' - The Strange Story of Ann Staight'. Also to Mr and Mrs Irvine for allowing me to use photographs of their home 'The Villa' and other photographs from the book.

Chapter Four- Dumbleton Hall – The House and Gardens

Verey D., (2002) The Buildings of England – Gloucestershire 2: The Vale and the Forest of Dean, Yale University Press.

OD Maps showing Dumbleton in 1833 and 1923.

Information and family photograph of George Percy Bankart by consent of his great granddaughter Marguerite Salter©

'Mr George Bankart and his work', Grey Wornum, The Architect's Journal, 12th October 1927)

Chapter Five – The Eyres-Monsell Family and Additions to the Hall

'The Listening Post' the newsletter of the Western Front Association, Worcestershire and Herefordshire Branch- August 2013.

With thanks to Mr Philip Manning and the Church of St Olave's, Hart Street London for allowing me to use the magnificent photograph of the Monsell Memorial Window for the book and for a fine colour plate.

To Mr Martin Purches and his Mother who was a 'Land Girl' at Dumbleton in World War 2- a very much appreciated thank you for the splendid photographs and the interview notes which Martin has asked his Mother for on her memories of the Hall at this time.

The National Portrait Gallery in London for their permission to include photographs for this chapter.

Chapter Six – Stories and Legends Associated with Dumbleton Hall and the Village

The 4900 Class locomotive 'Dumbleton Hall':- courtesy of the South Devon Railway Society©
The National Archives in London hold copies of his wartime dispatches from occupied Crete in file number HS 5/728 which make for some interesting reading.

Patrick Michael Leigh Fermor by Mark Gerson in February 1954:- courtesy of the NPG©

'In Tearing Haste – Letters between Deborah Devonshire and Patrick Leigh Fermor'

Chapter Seven- The Church and the Village of Dumbleton

Thanks to Mr Adrian Phillips and the *Dumbleton Society,* also the late Don Caisey with permission from Mrs Caisey to include a magnificent collection of photographs and postcards of the Church and the village of Dumbleton.

Mr Adrian Phillips who has given me so much support and kindly checked the chapters for me. His notes and articles on the Village and the 'Old Rectory' have been important.

Thanks to Mr and Mrs Oliver from 'The Old Rectory' for an outline of the history of this building.

Mr Finch from No 8. Main Street Dumbleton, for showing me his cottage and the baker's oven.

Mr Charles Matthews the Churchwarden and the Reverend Nick Carter the Vicar of Dumbleton for their support.

To thank Mr and Mrs Irvine of 'The Villa,' for permission to include some of the photographs of their home in the village.

The use of 'Lands Called Dumbleton' originally by J. C. L. Ellis-Mitchell, and revised in 1986 by the Revd Peter Richards. These little books have been incredibly useful in the writing of this chapter.

References to a variety of sources which have helped with this chapter have included:

Ellis-Mitchell J. C. L (undated) 'Lands Called Dumbleton' & the revised version of this booklet by Richards P. (1994) – The Revd Peter Richards, Rector of Dumbleton until 1994.

Atkyns, Sir Robert (1712): *The ancient and present state of Gloucestershire* – which contains the Kip's engravings.

Morris, Richard K. (1992): - City of Hereford Archaeology Unit – 'The Old Rectory, Dumbleton, Gloucestershire (Hereford Archaeology Series 149) & Mr Adrian Philips for his really useful history notes on the Rectory at Dumbleton.

Colvin H. (1995) – biography on the brothers Hurlbutt found in 'The Biographical Dictionary of British Architects' 1600-1840 – Yale University Press.

Somers Cocks J. V. (1988/9): 'The Cocks family of Dumbleton' (unpublished monograph).

David Hayton 1988: Sir Richard Cocks (c1659 - 1726) (a manuscript chapter from The History of Parliament.

Kingsley R. (1992) The Country Houses of Gloucestershire Vol.2: 1660-1830 (English Country Houses Series).

Rob and Pam Miffin for their support for my research on the brickyard at Dumbleton and their pictures and background to the site.

Susan Oldacre 'The Blacksmith's Daughter' with its view of Dumbleton during the time of Edward Holland and an insight into the 'Staight' family who were blacksmiths at Dumbleton for many years and also the butchers. Susan Oldacre is Susan Sinnott who kindly gave me her permission to dip into her splendid book.

Mrs Karen Morris and the Village Hall Committee for their support and interesting history and photographs of the village Hall.

The Head teacher and staff at Oakhill Primary School in the village for their support for this chapter of the book.

Richard Simpton who runs the Village shop in the Main Street of the village for always being supportive and always so hospitable on my various visits to the village for my research.

Chapter Eight- The Post Office Fellowship of Remembrance

To Mr Martin Grafton the archivist of Dumbleton Hall and one of the directors of the Post Office Fellowship of Remembrance who still own the Hall for his support and use of his research materials for the writing of this book. I am extremely grateful to him for this. To the support of the Hotel Staff at Dumbleton Hall Hotel, especially the manager Mr Gavin Dron and Mr Simon Kelly who have always made me welcome to the hotel and given me free access to take notes and photographs of the Hotel and the grounds.

Thanks are given for the support and encouragement of the Board of the Post Office Fellowship of Remembrance CIC owners of Dumbleton Hall which include the Chairman Mr Alan Bealby, the vice Chairman Jenny Cole and the directors Mr Martyn Bunn. Mr Tom Daffurn, Mr Ernie Dudley, Mr Brian Fox, Mr Martin Grafton, Mr Paul Mason, Mrs Debbie Terry and the Company Secretary Mr Simon Kelly.

In conclusion I would like to thank all those people who have come forward to help and encourage me with the writing of this book. I have had contacts from many people who have offered their memories, articles, diaries and photographs which have been invaluable to my research. If there is anyone who feels I have forgotten to mention them, personally please forgive me as your support is very much appreciated and your contribution is very highly valued and has made this book a little more interesting and personal. So a heartfelt thank you to you all, and I do hope you will enjoy this book.

....

'Dedicated in Memory of 12 850 GPO staff killed in two World Wars'

'For Our Tomorrows They Gave Their Today'